THE
GOOD
HUSBAND

HOW TO USE YOUR MASCULINE STRENGTHS
TO BENEFIT YOUR FAMLY

HAGAI AVISAR

Disclaimer

The ideas, suggestions, and practices provided in this book are of the nature of general guidance. They are not tailored to the specific circumstances and personalities of your family and not intended to replace professional help.

The author disclaims all responsibility and liability for any loss or damage allegedly arising from using the material in this book.

In memory of my father, who touched many with his humility and kindness.

CONTENTS

PART TWO
THE PRACTICE

WHY YOU SHOULD READ THIS BOOK

As a family man, I assume you aspire to create a healthy and happy home for your family. However, your experience raising children may have exposed a challenging reality that clashes with your initial dreams. Despite your good intentions and hard work, the ideals of a happy home may seem increasingly elusive.

This gap is frustrating and disillusioning. Men like you find themselves trying to cope with new demands, expectations, and rules around power and gender roles that our male ancestors never had to face. Without knowing how to cope, you may often find the marital experience distressing and challenging.

As a psychologist and couples therapist over the past thirty years, I have witnessed countless men who struggle to find solutions to relationship problems. As a result, they are often left feeling powerless and inadequate. Here is a sample of common problems I have heard:

- "I work hard to support my family and help around the house, but I keep hearing that something is not quite fair."
- "I regularly hear complaints and criticism."
- "I am puzzled by her changing moods and emotional reactions; they are increasingly hard to cope with."
- "I struggle to work out what she wants; she sounds vague and indecisive."
- "Nothing I do is ever good enough for her."
- "She is often angry, and I am unsure how to help."

- "Our sex life is nothing like what it was; her frequent rejections make me feel despair. As a result, I have stopped trying."
- "When I discipline the kids, she often interferes, not realizing how disempowering and hurtful this is."
- "I get worried when she spends too much money."
- "She jumps to threats of divorce and it scares me. I'm worried about losing access to my kids."

In the more extreme cases, I may hear nothing short of abuse stories, such as screaming, putting-downs, hitting, and throwing things.

How should you address such issues?

In the old days, men commonly resorted to forms of control, even violence, when challenged by their wives. Today, disengagement is their most common coping strategy. In the absence of skills to communicate effectively, negotiate solutions and settle differences, men feel a loss of power. In response, they tend to check out, shut down, and avoid. Their partners then feel even more frustrated and angry.

As the cycle worsens, men withdraw quietly into their grief and shame. They resign to that sense of helplessness and defeat. Some may develop symptoms of depression and anxiety, which are often masked by anger. To deal with feelings of despair and loneliness, some may escape to alcohol, drugs, pornography, or workaholism.

Sadly, these men often wake up too late and find themselves fighting the battle they dread the most—the fight in Family Court. Well-paid lawyers will advocate for them but can hardly guarantee decent access to their children. This tragic turn of events has a severe impact on both men's and women's mental health, as well as on the children's immediate well-being and how they grow up.

It should be obvious that men deserve support and education to fulfill their essential role in the family. Instead, men find themselves under attack, and their masculinity is regularly associated with negative terms, such as "toxic," "traditional," "patriarchal hierarchy," "male privilege," and more.

'Male bashing' has become a cultural trend that stems from the narrative of men being perpetrators and women being victims. Like toxins in the air, it infiltrates into marital drama and weakens a man's position in his family. Self-doubt and confusion then compromise a man's confidence to express himself, set boundaries, and fully use his authority.

When a man feels disempowered, shamed, and emasculated, his masculine strengths are suppressed and underutilized. Everyone loses. His wife finds herself disconnected, alone, and ever more frustrated and insecure in the relationship. Due to her pain, she may act out the behaviors mentioned above, hoping that her husband will respond to her needs. Although the last thing she needs is for him to check out, in the current social climate, he is powerless and confused. Both lose out.

Your reputation as a man may have been under cultural attack in recent times, but what I witness in my professional and personal life is a very different picture—men who are highly committed to their children and wives.

It is true that when it comes to their close relationships, men generally feel less competent compared to how they feel about their professional lives. Evolution has made men more naturally skilled as providers and protectors. Even if our biology is slow to catch up with the recent cultural changes, men can learn to adapt to these changes. This ability to adjust is how 'survival of the fittest' has worked throughout evolution. The fittest are the best learners. And what modern husbands want to learn is how to bring their masculine strengths into harmony with the relationship values of our culture.

Women's liberation is certainly a blessing, but in family life, women's gain of power has come at the expense of men's loss of power. This creates havoc in many relationships. We must correct this for the sake of our children and our society as a whole. This correction is a new paradigm that capitalizes on your masculine strengths to benefit your family, and what I set out to achieve with the *Good Husband* project.

Being a *Good Husband* is about serving your family. Any support provided to you is therefore also support for your family.

A positive new roadmap

To restore power to your roles as husband and father, you need a new roadmap to follow. A positive one! You want inspiration, not more opposition, condemnation, and shaming. Instead of being defensive and apologetic about your masculinity, you need to utilize the positive qualities associated with it, such as:

- courage,
- leadership,
- ambition,
- willingness to risk your life for others, and
- self-reliance.

Over time, these qualities have helped secure the freedom and prosperity many now take for granted. They can also help you consolidate your unique role as a man in your family. In this book, I will offer you an operating manual for aligning your healthy masculine instincts with the values of modern family life. It is a framework of thinking with practical tools to utilize your masculine power.

Power is your capacity to influence your family members. It is very different from control which often leads to resistance and, therefore to a loss of power. The word "influence" comes from the Latin word *influere*, meaning "in flow." and an indirect, imperceptible impact. Interestingly, the root of the word "influence" in Hebrew (my mother tongue) is abundance. When you try to influence members of your family, you want to operate from a place of 'flow' and 'abundance'—in simple terms, from your caring heart.

Based on thousands of my male clients, the picture is clear: They perceive their ideal self as being caring and protective men. When I ran a survey among my workshop participants to help me choose a name for the project, they selected *The Good Husband*. It reflected both their aspiration and what they hoped to learn.

"Good" might be incorrectly interpreted as being 'nice' or 'positive' towards your wife. This is not what I mean. There is a difference between 'being a good man' and 'being good at being a man.' When I say *Good Husband*, I mean being good at being a husband and manifesting your masculine strengths. The expression of your strengths is not always 'nice' in the conventional sense. For example, confronting family members and setting boundaries is not always nice and easy. But it is good when it serves a good purpose—the well-being of your family.

What's in it for you

This book offers you perspectives and tools that my clients find to be most useful for them. You can learn in this book what I normally cover with clients over a year of counseling. I speak to you plainly, man-to-man. Men generally love the no-nonsense approach with clear directions, useful tools, practical advice, and… challenges!

The book will support you in the following ways:

- On the moral level, you will feel acknowledged for your unique strengths and contributions as a man.
- On the emotional level, you will better understand the needs of both yourself and your wife, leading to less judgment and shame, as well as more acceptance.
- On the intellectual level, you will deepen your understanding of relationship issues and get new perspectives on your role in the family.
- On the practical level, you will find useful tools, strategies, and solutions to common relationship problems such as conflicts, loss of respect, threats of divorce, struggling sex life, criticism, and more.

In Part One of the book, you will begin to understand the roadmap for expressing your healthy masculinity. The model of *The Good Husband* is based on four classical masculine roles (archetypes):

- King
- Lover
- Magician
- Warrior

Each role comes with its own set of strengths and actions to exhibit.

Part Two of the book is all about the practice. This is your training ground. You will learn how to activate each of the four masculine roles through various practices and tools.

Language and cultural issues

Throughout this book is a generalization that it's the husband who fulfills the masculine role in the family. I believe that this role is equally aligned with a woman's biologically driven needs when she raises children. If not, I would not be writing this book. The healthy expression of masculinity contributes positively to the lives of both partners.

I mention it here because I am aware of the social sensitivity to the subject of men and power. The current cultural climate makes it hard to provide men with relationship guidance without the risk of upsetting some people. The discussion of gender roles is often loaded with passion and ideologies. Certain words may trigger different interpretations, different reactions, and strong feelings, and sadly when they do, we lose the ability to engage in a constructive conversation.

My humble aim is not to preach any ideology here, but to focus on **what works for couples** and to be as pragmatic as possible. I am neither pro-men nor pro-women. I am pro-family; I am pro-children. As a couples therapist, I am committed to both husbands and wives. Marriage is a story about connection, and the role of a couples therapist is to help partners maintain a strong connection while holding an empathic perspective towards their flaws and their struggles.

When I use the words "husband" and "marriage" in this book, I refer to men in committed relationships. I may interchangeably use terms such as "partner" and "spouse." I trust you not to let language issues compromise the benefits you will receive from reading the book and applying its tools.

My story

I grew up and studied clinical psychology in Tel Aviv, Israel. This is where I also met my wife Judy, who migrated from Melbourne, Australia. When our kids were 5 and 6, we moved to her hometown to be closer to her family.

After twenty-five years together and several ups and downs in our relationship, we reached a stage in which we had drifted apart, and the marriage was beyond repair. Our children were young adults, and the option of separation was viable and appropriate. I can gratefully say that our friendship and care for each other have remained strong.

I regard my long marriage as a corrective relationship experience that helped me heal from my traumatic childhood experience. At age eight, I was placed in an institution for children from dysfunctional families. I experienced abandonment and neglect, and along the way I honed my resilience and Warrior spirit. My marriage taught me that a partner could be your best psychotherapist. We heal through a secure and committed relationship.

I am grateful for a rewarding and meaningful marriage. Together we did good things for our families and our community. For example, in Israel, we helped set up a parent helpline, started a community of adoptive families for children of Ethiopian origin, and supported the Ethiopian community.

When a marriage is unraveling, it is often the result of many complex factors. Unfortunately, most of those factors are not known to us at the time. Only with the perspective of time can we realize our mistakes.

I wish I could say with pride that I did a good job using the tools I share with you in this book. I didn't. Wisdom and awareness grow over time. I would have done things differently had I known what I understand now. But I have no regrets if I can pass on the insights and tools I desperately needed at the time.

And if you wonder about my 'hero journey' from that powerless child in an institution to where I am today, I believe you can find the answer somewhere within and between the lines of this book.

PART ONE

UNDERSTANDING THE GOOD HUSBAND MODEL

1
THE CHALLENGE

"It seems we have arrived at a point in our evolutionary development where men must reject out of hand their manlier instincts in favor of more 'womanly' traits... Men who play to their masculine strengths are seen as problematic, dysfunctional, or oppressive."

— James Innes-Smith, The Death of Masculinity

We live in times of confusion and tension around gender roles and how they manifest themselves in family life. The old order of gender roles served the survival of our species for thousands of generations. However, the old order became dysfunctional in an evolutionary instant, and we are struggling to settle into the new order.

It has only been one hundred years since women started to participate in the democratic process, making their mark in politics, the workplace, and academia. Women's empowerment in our culture has blessed us all with an increased expression of values such as justice, compassion, equality, and honesty, and it has also impacted family life. Contemporary wives and husbands have a new set of expectations around their respective family roles. Our families, however, are also where our emotions, hormones, and attachments play key roles. This is where the gap between biology and culture hits us hard—the gap between the harsh reality of our ancient instincts and the values of our modern culture. This gap is nowhere as pronounced or potentially tragic as during the raising of young children.

Most couples today raise their children in isolation. They live in cities where there is limited local community contact that are often miles away from their hometowns. The old saying is that "It takes a village to raise a child," but that village has long gone. This means that when babies arrive, you are that 'village' for your wife and babies. You are the main support. That is one hell of a big mission, and it's brand new in terms of evolution. You are not naturally equipped with the tools to address all of her emotional and physical needs during these early stressful years of parenting. The females in her life would surely do a better job, but now it is all on you, and you may struggle to respond properly to her needs. During stressful times, your wife's emotional reactivity may be very hard to take, particularly when it comes to anger and blame. It can leave you feeling inadequate and powerless. There is really no one to blame for this tragic gap between the demands on you both and your scarce resources.

As a society, we naturally want to provide empathy and support to mothers who struggle with raising babies. But what about young fathers? How much understanding and empathy do they receive? Not much at all. In the case of Warren Farrell, it even proved risky to offer empathy to men. As a social researcher, author, and women's rights activist in the 70s and 80s, Farrell was the darling of the feminists. But in the 90s, when he turned his attention to men's sacrifices and advocated for their rights, their attitude towards him changed into hostility.[1]

But Farrell has remained heroic in his advocacy for all members of the family. Together with John Gray, he published a seminal work in 2018—*The Boy Crisis*[2]—which tells the very sad story of children who grow up without fathers. With a significant amount of research data, the authors show how fatherless boys suffer the consequences of low achievement, serious mental health issues, troubled relationships, criminal activity, and suicide. Together with these children, we as a society pay a heavy price when men fail to be there for their children.

Men deserve our moral and professional support while handling the super complex task of raising a young family. But managing without support is one type of challenge; managing in a cultural climate of shaming and emasculating men is quite another.

The attack on masculinity

Attacking masculinity has become a social trend. Some of the attacks are more direct and explicit, as you see in the media,[3] while others are more sophisticated and disguised as gender studies in academia.[4] The hostile attitude towards masculine identity reached a unique milestone in 2018 with the publication of the *Guidelines for Psychological Practice with Boys and Men* by the American Psychology Association. The APA is a hugely influential institution with more than one hundred twenty thousand members and it impacts practitioners, educators, and policymakers. Their document warns that traditional masculinity is psychologically harmful for men. Do you wonder what they mean by "traditional"? Here are some of the traits they add to this psychologically harmful basket: achievement, adventure, risk, emotional stoicism, not showing vulnerability, self-reliance, and competitiveness.[5]

Stoicism? This is the endurance and acceptance of hardships without displaying feelings and without complaining. It is a noble trait valued by most cultures around the world. I am certainly proud of my stoicism.

Self-reliance? This means that you are not inclined to seek help from therapists like myself. (Shame on you...).

Competitiveness, dominance, and aggression? Such traits are highly valuable in certain contexts such as business, sport, protecting your family, and fighting for your country.

I trust that you share with me the pain of getting such a message from a body that is supposed to care for people, men included. Find comfort in the fact that the backlash to these ideology-driven guidelines was strong and swift.[6,7,8]

Why did a body like the APA publish such an unfortunate message?

When you read the whole document, you realize that the authors are driven by a politically progressive agenda that aims to address issues of privilege and power. They truly want to change the world. One of the authors said, "If we can change men, we can change the world."[9] Now you have the reason why it was published—the authors want to change you.

How?

They expose your "masculine ideology" and challenge you to change this harmful ideology by thinking differently about your gender role. They argue that your masculine traits have nothing to do with biological instincts and evolutionary forces. Instead, they are all in your mind, conditioned

by language and cultural beliefs. I trust you sigh while reading this distorted view.

But the authors were not only concerned about saving the world. They were also motivated by the urgent need to find some cure for the many troubled men who suffer from social isolation, poor health, substance and alcohol abuse, violence, and suicide. Their intentions were good, but blaming their clients for their "ideology" is a catastrophic failure in understanding how men operate and what men need to be their best. They certainly don't need more shaming.

The cultural bug

This shortcut to fixing your masculinity through changing your "ideology"—how you think—is a symptom of what I call the "cultural bug." I often use the term "mental bug" in my counseling work to describe a uniquely dysfunctional thinking pattern. It acts like a bug because it is hardly noticeable, but it harms mental health the same way a virus harms the body. The cultural bug is a form of mental bug. Like many others in the field of social science, the authors of the APA document were victims of this cultural bug.

For this *Good Husband* project, you should be acutely aware of this bug and its insidious impact on all relevant aspects of your family life. Particularly how it may sabotage your position and confidence as a man in your family. So let me elaborate a little about it.

The cultural bug is the tendency to enforce ideology on reality and science. The 'progressive' ideology of social justice clashes with the reality of the innate differences between men and women. The contradiction between the 'real and the ideal' is unsettling, so people tend to resist and bend reality to match the ideals. Facts, truth, and science get in their way, so they sacrifice them on the altar of their desired ideals. Such a distortion is very common in the discussion about gender identity. This 'ideology' is ultimately not 'traditional masculinity,' but is in the minds of some ideologists who have turned their fight for equality into a war on men and masculinity.

But if you want equality, why attack masculinity? This attempt to demolish masculinity looks like an overreaction by some women to the threat they perceive from men. Lack of protection from male partners only exacerbates this anxiety. Many years ago, when paranoid men perceived women as a threat, they started a witch-hunt and burned thousands of women at the stake. The female version of a witch-hunt against men is the academic articles and online blogs against masculinity. This is not as dramatic and bloody at first glance, but it has severe ramifications for the health and security of our free society.

Here are some of the symptoms of the cultural bug:

Political correctness (PC)

Political correctness operates on these two assumptions:

1. Reality is subjective and only exists in our minds in the form of interpretations, narratives, and meaning.
2. Since our mind operates by language, if we change language, we change reality. Simple.

PC tells us how we should or shouldn't speak to avoid offending members of particular groups. In practice, it is used to penalize how we speak. Just as some Muslim men force women to cover their bodies so that men are not sexually triggered by them, PC advocates try to 'cover' our mouths so that they are not upset by our words and ideas. A local organization rejected my workshops for husbands and this is how their email explained it: "that would potentially exclude members of our community... We try to be as open and inclusive as possible and avoid hetero-normative or gender binary."

Men are bastards

'Men bashing' has become an acceptable form of expression in the media. In an analysis of the content of two thousand media articles and program segments, researcher Jim Macnamara from the University of Technology Sydney found that men are often portrayed in the mass media as villains, aggressors, perverts, and philanderers. Macnamara warns of "the trend towards demonizing, marginalizing, and trivializing of men and male identity."[10] In their book *Spreading Misandry: The Teaching of Contempt for Men in Popular Culture*, Paul Nathanson and Katherine Young try to raise awareness of this disturbing, sad, and insidious phenomenon.[11] This form of hatred towards men doesn't stop in the media and academia. It harms the harmony in our society and sadly affects the dynamics of marital relationships as well as the status of fatherhood in divorce cases.

Gender is a social construct

Gender studies (researched and taught primarily by women) are out to prove that our gender differences are not biological but almost entirely cultural. Accepting this notion means that if only society educates you correctly and changes your perceptions and expectations of gender roles, then the forces of evolution will magically move out of the way. It creates confusion between biological reality and cultural ideals. Google's chief executive suffered from this confusion when he sacked a senior employee who "offended" female employees by suggesting that "preferences and abilities of men and women differ in part due to biological causes."[12]

Imagine the troubles I would get into if I argued that we have more women than men in my counseling profession because the male brain is better able to deal with 'things' than people. The critical difference is that as a male reader you won't be offended by such a statement, let alone protest it. The cultural bug has created an environment where it is safe to state facts that are not flattering to men, but not safe to state facts that may be interpreted as offensive to women.

Now consider the enormous bias in reporting such facts in science and the media. Men and the truth are paying the price. You can assume that your wife is affected one way or another by this bias.

Female victimhood narrative

Never in human history have females had so much freedom and power. Yet the dominant narrative remains the same old story: women are the victims, and men are their perpetrators. It's not hard to imagine how such a narrative can pit men and women against each other, particularly within the dynamics of marriage. Occasionally we hear a woman who dares to condemn the victimhood mentality, as in the case of Jess Butcher in her TED Talk "Is modern feminism starting to undermine itself?"[13]

Marriage as a patriarchal institution

Some feminists regard marriage as an oppressive patriarchal institution in which men exercise their power over women. They also regard divorce as liberation. Not only is such an ideology aggressively biased against men, but it is also most damaging to children.[14] Coercion control in relationships was the topic of an article in a professional magazine distributed to all psychologists in Australia. The author was probably tired of disguising her aggression towards the end. With a cynical tone, she concluded that "many men do not presume or want dominance in their relationships."[15] Sadly, this is the kind of subtle toxicity you often see in both the media and academia.

The impact of the cultural bug

I witness the impact in my clinic every day. Men are afraid to express their masculinity. They are confused about what is expected of them. Confusion makes them avoidant and hesitant. They stop responding authentically as men. Inauthentic men are non-assertive, immature, aggressive, moody, unreliable, dependent, and passive. No wonder they end up hearing from their women—"man up!" The vacuum they create is filled by combative wives who argue like lawyers over matters of power, fairness, control, etc.

The absence of masculine energy creates a void that only makes the situation worse and further frustrates these wives. Many partners now find themselves in a vicious spiral: If the wife's high expectations are not met, she often gets frustrated (and increasingly demanding and blaming). In response, her husband may withdraw even more while she gets more frustrated and aggressive. Tragically, the void then grows bigger.

If you attend couples counseling, you will most likely see a female therapist. It is reasonable to assume that she may be affected by the cultural bug and the APA Guidelines about your 'masculine ideology.' When my partner and I attended marriage counseling some years ago, it took the female counselor only 20 minutes to diagnose me as "controlling." However, when I asked her for examples of what made her form such an impression so quickly, she went silent! I instantly left the room feeling humiliated and hurt. That was the cultural bug in action.

Domestic violence is another area where the cultural bug affects men. Men face a hostile attitude from the justice system even when clearly not at fault. Based on her 13 years experience in the police force, one female police officer says that more than half of the violent incidents she knew of were instigated by women (2021).[16] Men suffer from abuse by their partners, mostly psychological, but it is under-reported. This is one of the serious consequences of men being emasculated and afraid to assert their boundaries. For many men, the need for assertiveness is a matter of urgency. They need to restore the qualities of a Warrior (Details in Chapter Seven).

Men who are watching and feeling the impact of the cultural bug are also becoming more wary of committing to marriage. American psychologist Helen Smith has described this phenomenon in her book *Men on Strike*. She argues that men avoid marriage for good reasons: they lose power, have less sex, lose respect, and risk losing their children, money, space, and freedom.[17] The vicious spiral of anger—avoidance then more anger and more avoidance is now shaping up in the level of society. No one wins from this ideology-driven tension between the two genders. Angry feminists who attack masculinity make both genders lose.

Women have been feeling unsafe in this world for too long and their hurt should of course be validated. After all, as good men, we want to protect our sisters, daughters and wives from any sick men. We, as men, have suffered from them as well. Sadly, with the social trend to condemn masculinity, men are being robbed of core qualities of their identity which help protect women, such as being brave, assertive, and competitive. The baby is being thrown away together with the dirty water.

This book is trying to keep the baby alive and kicking.

The cultural anti-bug

Thankfully, there is a battle being waged against the cultural bug. The cultural anti-bug aims for the return of wisdom and truth for the sake of men, women, and children. Unsung heroes—both male and female—are at the forefront of this battle. Many of them are well-known psychologists and authors who safeguard the reputation of my psychology profession. Others are women who speak against anti-male feminism. You can watch many of them on Ted Talks and YouTube channels, such as Bettina Arndt. With their sharp minds and strong voices, they show courage in the fight against the cultural bug—and at times they pay a price.

They expose how these so-called "progressive ideas" destroy reason, science, and rational debate. For example, in their book *Cynical Theories*, Helen Pluckrose and James Lindsay brilliantly explain how our universities are the breeding ground for this bug and how it affects social science researchers and harms everybody.[18] Other scholars who expose the cultural bug include Warren Farrell, Jordan Peterson, Steven Pinker, Jonathan Haidt, Sam Harris, Gad Saad, and many others.

One female hero deserves special mention—Dr. Carole Hooven. She shares enlightening facts and encouraging messages from her field of evolutionary biology in her research and teaching at Harvard University. Her book *T: The Story of Testosterone, the Hormone that Dominates and Divides Us* was published while I was writing this book.[19] Her insights convey empathy and understanding, which is the kind of attitude men are seeking from women. When they come from a woman like Dr. Carole Hooven, who has been a victim of rape, these messages carry additional power and insights. With profound wisdom, she writes that "Testosterone pushes the psychology and behavior of the sexes apart...Understanding the forces that drive us helps to equip us to combat the expression of the darker parts of our nature."

While sharing her scientific data, Dr. Hooven laments the limits to free speech and the perils she has experienced in the current cultural bug environment. She strongly advocates to keep the noise out of science and to see the truth as it is. "I have a better understanding of male nature, the power of culture, and how we can work as a society to support men in learning to control some of the darker aspects of their nature, always while holding them accountable for their behavior..." In an interview for The Australian, she said that the answer is "not to hate men or the testosterone that runs in their blood."[20]

Further, she acknowledges the good men who have helped her throughout her life. "It's been mostly the men in my life who have supported me and encouraged me to follow my dreams. To go for things I didn't think I could accomplish, ...men, far more than women, risk their own lives to save the lives of others."

Dr. Hooven is truly inspirational.

Winning for both genders

"We are all rowing the same family boat. Between the sexes, there is no such thing as 'winning.' Whenever only one sex wins, both sexes lose."

— Warren Farrell and John Gray, The Boy Crisis

For both genders to win, we need to fix the advocacy and empathy gap. Women are doing an excellent job advocating for their sisters, as well as for other social justice matters. The victims' need to be heard is met by highly capable and empathic women. Unfortunately, men and women don't match this level of caring when it comes to male suffering and sacrifice. For a start, men themselves tend to avoid complaining. Many struggle to even articulate their feelings and needs. They don't like to appear as victims. Further, men tend to challenge, compete, or criticize each other, rather than share empathy and understanding. The end result is the empathy gap. Men as a group are left without a proper response to the cultural bug. We need to correct it.

In the history of the human race, when the dark side of masculinity has taken over, men have left a trail of blood, death, and destruction behind them. However, civilization has survived thanks to other courageous men who stopped the carnage. As the tide of history is turning towards the full expression of feminine power, it's possible that we are witnessing its dark side as well—confusion, denial, self-righteousness, and victimhood. If that is the case, let's hope more courageous women and men come to their senses and work together to arrest and contain it. We want to live in a society where both masculine and feminine strengths are celebrated and both men and women are met with empathy for their flaws and struggles.

Meeting the challenge

Restoring your constructive masculine power is essential to your mental health, your family's welfare, and the welfare of society as a whole. Loss of power breeds rage, depression, nihilism, and antisocial behaviors. Your position as husband and father might have been weakened by various forces such as the cultural bug, but there is still much you can do to strengthen it. You have the power to learn, upskill, build your character, and shape your future. When you do, it's your ultimate freedom.

I live this belief every day through my profession and my personal life. As a child, I grew up in conditions of poverty. I had a dysfunctional family, and I was raised in an institution from the age of 8 until I was 14. I had to learn to cope with life's challenges the hard way. Victimhood was never an option for me. I developed resilience by overcoming obstacles and hardships, one at a time. My strong sense of agency—'it is all up to me'—has been my life-saving mantra. It all begins with owning our thoughts and behaviors. I suggest this is the place for you to start too.

Let's wise up!

My clients often tell me that the most helpful input I offer them is a fresh perspective. This perspective is grounded in reality, human experience, and scientific research. When you see things differently, you respond differently. Wisdom is about taking a pragmatic approach that works. The perspectives and tools you will learn in this book will prepare and hopefully inspire you to take action and reclaim your constructive masculine power in your family.

Our action plan will include clarifying your role, redefining your masculine power, and putting your masculine potential into practice. If it's not used to love and build, this potential might be used to hurt and destroy. The premise of this book is that your authentic and mature masculine power is a force for good, and you are encouraged to acknowledge, embrace, and use this power to benefit your family.

Let's turn now to explore your masculine strengths!

2
MASCULINE STRENGTHS

"We need to learn to love and be loved by the mature Masculine. We need to learn to celebrate authentic masculine power and potency, for the sake of our personal wellbeing and for our relationships."

— Robert Moore and Douglas Gillette,
King, Warrior, Magician, Lover

When bullets rained over the crowd in the Las Vegas massacre of 2017, killing fifty-eight, men covered women with their bodies to save their lives. Rather than using feelings or words, men tend to show their relationship strengths through their actions, including risking their lives to protect and save their family, working hard, fixing problems, and offering practical help, no matter the risk to their own well-being. On the other hand, women tend to express their feminine strengths through relating, caring, nurturing, and more.

Before we explore masculine strengths, it is important to keep in mind that these typical expressions of masculine and feminine strengths are **not** mutually exclusive.[21] It is desirable for men to cultivate certain feminine strengths (such as empathy) and for women to cultivate certain masculine strengths (such as assertiveness). For example, I personally absorbed warmth and compassion from my father, not my mother.

View feminine strengths as complementary assets that you can tap into. They should not come at the expense of your masculinity. In fact, feminine strengths will give you more (not less) confidence in your masculinity. Why? Because balancing your masculine and feminine traits will boost your mental health, strengthen your social adjustment, and expand your character. When men and women tap into both masculine and feminine strengths, they experience wholeness and better health.

Gender roles in the family context

Family life (and in particular, the experience of raising young children) is a unique context where masculine and feminine roles tend to be expressed based on the traditional gender roles—you act as a provider and protector, while your wife acts as a caretaker and nurturer. For the survival of the species, we follow the evolutionary instincts required for raising our offspring. These are our sexual, relational, and parenting instincts. They are so deep and powerful in how they impact our behaviors when we raise families that many of the socially constructed beliefs and expectations about gender roles must be adjusted. Evolutionary psychologist David Buss explains: "Men and women differ in their psychology of mating solely and specifically in the domains where they have faced recurrently different adaptive problems over the long course of evolution."[22]

Motherhood is a compelling and formative task in your wife's life. Her vulnerabilities and needs during the early parenting experience will adjust and require adjustment from you as well. This adjustment is how evolution shaped your masculine strengths to a large degree. These are the times when gender-role behaviors are clearly demarcated. A few examples (my generalization here is to reflect typical stories and obviously not the case for all couples):

- she is immersed in child rearing, and you in breadwinning;
- she is seeking support, reassurance, and emotional connection, while you are seeking appreciation, sexual satisfaction, and fulfilment that comes from making her happy;
- she worries about rejection, fitting in socially, and body image, while you worry about performance, money, failure, and shame;
- she criticizes or complains, while you withdraw and avoid;
- she interprets some of your behaviors as a lack of care towards her, while you take her complaints to mean that you are not good enough;
- she is softer on the kids, and you tougher; and
- an affair for her is an attempt to meet emotional needs; for you, it is about sexual needs.

And the list goes on. World-renowned relationship researcher John Gottman says "Gender differences are clearly important in understanding how marriages function and dysfunction."[23]

Gender differences

To research masculine strengths, I have looked at literature on gender differences,[24,25] evolutionary psychology,[26] masculinity,[27,28] and gender in marriage.[29,30]

The concepts of masculinity and femininity are complex and create controversy among researchers. Do we agree that there are traits innately typical to men and women, or is this perception all in our head? Is it about nature (e.g., genes and hormones) or social environment (e.g., parenting, peers, and culture)?

So much passion and ideology (i.e., the cultural bug) is driving researchers in this field that at times it is hard to 'see the forest from the trees.' Richard Lippa, in his comprehensive book *Gender, Nature, and Nurture*, helps us to gain some clarity about how and why men and women are different.[31] The conclusion is that researchers should ultimately follow common sense—nature **and** nurture make us who we are.

It is best to see these gender differences as two types of intelligence—masculine and feminine. Through evolution, men and women specialized in tasks that helped them survive. These tasks shaped in them unique capacities. Protecting and providing led men to the development of masculine intelligence, which is about being instrumental, goal-oriented, and focused on the external world of work. It includes traits such as independence, assertiveness, determination, focus, dominance, and leadership. Raising children and building a network of social support led women to the development of feminine intelligence, which is about being relational, expressive, people-oriented ,and focused on family and personal relationships. It includes traits such as nurturing, warmth, empathy, sensitivity to others, and agreeableness. As a family man, you surely value and benefit from your wife's feminine intelligence, and you hope she values and benefits from your masculine intelligence.

Based on the various resources I mentioned above, I have compiled in Table 1 some key differences between feminine and masculine intelligence.

Key gender differences

	Masculine	Feminine
Evolutionary purpose	provide and protect	reproduce and raise babies
Primal needs	to feel appreciated, sexually fulfilled, respected, valued	to feel secure, desired, connected, and supported
Expression	do, perform, act	connect, nurture, feel, be attractive
Self-worth is affected by	performance, achievement	relationships, appearance, body image
Values	individual rights and freedom, self-expression, accomplishment	care for others, justice, equality, community, serving others
Interest	things	people
Traits	goal-oriented, focused on the external world of work, independence, assertiveness, dominance, leadership	people-oriented, focused on the private worlds of family and personal relationships, warmth, empathy, sensitivity to others
In conflicts	assertive	agreeable
Communication style	direct, succinct, instrumental	indirect, elaborative, emotional
Vulnerability	anger, aggression	anxiety, moods
Threats in marriage	failure, shame	rejection, loss of connection

The expression of these two types of intelligence can be highly influenced by individuals, context, and culture. For example, if your nation is busy fighting an enemy, you can expect more men to display the masculine traits of a warrior. If women aim at higher positions in their careers, they will display the masculine traits of assertiveness and leadership. The same principle applies to men in the context of modern marriage: to adapt to the new norms and support their families, men need to tap into their relational and feminine intelligence such as caring, sensitivity, and connection.

Interestingly, the differences in how men and women express their gender intelligence are bigger when a society is open and free. Men and women authentically express their innate masculine/feminine traits when free from cultural pressure and shame. As you can imagine, this fact doesn't sit well with the cultural bug because it leads to different career paths for men and women. This in turn results in different financial outcomes, in which females are attracted to 'people jobs' where the pay is lower than in 'things jobs.' Must we blame someone for this inequality?

Another interesting impact we find when we look at how masculine and feminine traits predict coping and mental health of people. Researchers assessed both sets of traits and correlated them with measures of adjustment and self-esteem. It turns out that men **and** women who scored higher on masculinity traits also scored higher on measures of adjustment, and lower on anxiety and depression. So masculinity in fact predicts adjustment better than femininity based on the findings of this study. The researchers called this impact "the masculine superiority effect."[32] They explained that in the context of an individualistic free enterprise society, masculine traits, such as assertiveness, competitiveness, self-directedness, and leadership, foster success. One could guess, that if they measured levels of social engagement and family connectedness women would have done better.

In this book, we look at gender differences with an attitude of acceptance and compassion. We understand that the arrival of children unleashes the evolutionary forces that have helped the human race survive. These forces make us display our innate differences in strengths and vulnerabilities. These differences mean that we must treat each other 'uniquely,' rather than 'equally.' They also mean that certain behaviors will not have the same impact on the opposite sex. For example, her anger towards you is not the same as your anger towards her, her avoiding you is not the same as you avoiding her, and her 'no' to sex is not like your 'no' to her bid for sex. Throughout the book, you will see this 'double standard' time and again. I mention it only to encourage awareness and acceptance. It is not a moral judgment.

The premise of our program is that we accept and embrace differences in personalities, rather than fight them. Only then can we begin to exercise our strengths and work effectively with our vulnerabilities.

Masculinity in its glory and tragedy

The documentary *The Rescue* tells the breath-taking and heroic story about the rescue of a soccer team of 12 boys and their coach who got stuck in a cave in Thailand. The story shows masculinity in both its glory and tragedy. A group of male cave divers comes from far away to risk their lives to save others in a remote part of the world. As the story unfolds, you witness with awe their courage, focus, determination, and kindness. Your awe doesn't prepare you for their reflections on their personal lives. These heroes have experienced in their life social awkwardness and aloofness. Some have struggled with close relationships, and even suffered from bullying and shaming. One of the cave divers reflects on his weakness: "as a cold unemotional man, I found a use and a purpose to that level of detachment. You can use it to do good things."[33]

Do you believe these men were driven by their "masculine ideology" as the American psychologists' guidelines suggest? And what was the "ideology"?! To risk your life to save others? or perhaps to shut off emotions?

One thing is certain: at least 13 women are grateful to have such men around us.

Your masculine strengths

The following masculine strengths are relevant to *The Good Husband* project. They are not only 'natural' to being masculine, but also what females seek in a male partner and the father of their children.

"I provide"

Evolutionary psychology is the study of how evolution has shaped the way we think and behave. According to this body of research, males evolved in their masculinity to meet female demands for resources. These are the resources she needs to fulfill the mission that nature endowed—to reproduce and raise babies.

International and cross-cultural studies prove that women expect partner strengths that are likely to guarantee security, access to resources, stability, and good parenting. Examples include:

- ambition,
- industriousness,
- leadership,
- intelligence,
- dependability,
- emotional stability, and
- kindness.

Interestingly, when women have a higher status, their expectations from a mating partner don't change! This further proves that our ancient instincts are stronger than the present cultural norms.

"I protect"

Safety has been a massive concern for females throughout history and across all cultures. It continues to be. Being vulnerable and the object of desire, females are potentially exposed to physical attacks from males. Studies on mating behaviors show that females value male partner characteristics like courage, assertiveness, and physical strength to help protect them and set clear boundaries that other males should not cross.[34]

If our opposite sex expects us to behave in a certain way, we tend to exhibit this behavior. This is what we find when we study perceptions and expectations. A review of sex differences in personality traits across 26 cultures showed that men are perceived as more assertive, dominant, competitive, and direct, while women are more submissive and nurturing.[35]

The Carnegie Medal is a heroism award given every year to people in the US and Canada who have faced extreme danger while trying to save the lives of others. Nearly every year, more than 95% of recipients are men. Many have sacrificed their lives to save others.[36]

"I am a leader"

Leadership is a trait which is associated with masculinity. To lead, you need to be resolved, decisive, determined, and clear in your vision and goals. When men express leadership, they do so mostly via their societal roles outside the family. Through these roles, they gain a social status that reflects their achievement, success, influence, and power. A male's social status is very appealing to females because it is a strong cue for access to resources.[37]

"I am honorable"

One large international study of more than twenty-seven thousand men in Germany, the US, the UK, Spain, Brazil, Mexico, Italy, and France found that being self-reliant, respected, and seen as "a man of honor" that is "in control of your own life" were their most important traits defining masculinity.[38] Honor and respect do not imply preoccupation with one's ego, but with one's rights and responsibilities. This honor is your unique place in society, unique talent, and contribution. You and your family members are worthy of unconditional honor.

"I am stoic"

As outlined in Chapter One, according to the shameful APA guidelines, stoicism is not a virtue but something we should fix. Well, your wife and children would disagree with that. They want you to display emotional regulation and remain centered and measured during turbulent times. The ability to 'hold up' under pressure and tolerate pain are important aspects of the stoic masculine strength. Stoicism will be reflected in masculine traits such as being:

- objective,
- not easily influenced,
- logical,
- able to separate feelings from ideas,
- not panicking in a minor crisis, and
- not easily hurt.

A male's innate ability to disidentify and keep some distance from emotional stimuli can be helpful in managing stressful family matters. Disidentify means that the emotional drama with the kids does not define your identity or worthiness. For mothers it is harder to create such a distance. Further, a male's drive to systemize and analyze helps to observe the drama and keep emotions under control. Obviously, if taken to the extreme, this ability may become a liability. For example, it is not helpful for men to appear emotionally disconnected and aloof.

"I am the agent of change"

Agency is the capacity to exert power. The opposite is victimhood. A sense of agency means believing in your ability to control your own goals, actions, and destiny. You believe that what happens to you begins with you. Examples of agentic behaviors are:

- self-motivating,
- self-organizing,
- self-reflecting, and
- any self-directed behavior aimed at achieving your goals.

Surveys about desirable traits reveal a gender-based pattern: for men it is desirable to show higher agency and for women to show higher relatability. This difference had remained stable since 1974, when the masculine/feminine measure was developed.[39] Men show masculine traits associated with agency by being:

- independent,
- strong,
- decisive,
- competitive,
- driven,
- self-confident,
- determined,
- ambitious,
- tough,
- active, and
- able to 'hold up' under pressure.

"I am goal-oriented"

On its deepest level, a male's approach to tasks reflects his sexual behaviors. Males tend to be strategists and goal-focused, while females tend to focus on processes and relationships. Researchers call the masculine style "instrumental-goal-oriented" and the feminine "expressive-emotional."[40] As a goal-oriented male, you focus on getting the job done, fixing things, and solving the problem. You are a doer.

Masculine strengths and the Model of The Good Husband

As a man, you may relate to some or most of these masculine strengths but wonder how they help you in the context of your marriage. You need a roadmap to put them into practice in your marriage. That's why I created *The Good Husband* model which I present in the next chapter. I adopted the inspiring story of the four male ancient roles—archetypes—in developing this model:

- KING,
- LOVER,
- MAGICIAN,
- WARRIOR.

As you can see in the table, various masculine strengths converge to form each of these roles.

The four roles and their masculine strengths

KING	LOVER	MAGICIAN	WARRIOR
leader-like	desiring a woman	stoic	providing
honorable	goal-oriented	objective	protecting
has integrity	caring for family	data-oriented	assertive
keeps his word	committed	dispassionate	goal-oriented
dependable	fun-loving	perspective-taking	sense of agency
focused	humorous	critical thinking	ambitious
providing			competitive
protecting			decisive

These roles are virtually classic characters that you see in movies and books. The ability to **identify** with each of the roles gives the model its power. By the very process of getting into the role you will find yourself exhibiting the strengths associated with it. As you learn to operate each role like an actor, your masculine strengths will become your assets.

It is time to learn *The Good Husband* model!

3
THE GOOD HUSBAND MODEL

*"**Hold her**. Hold her when you are dating. Hold her when you are married. Hold her when she's upset. Hold her when she's happy. Hold her when she is scared. Hold her when she feels unworthy of being held and hold her when she's mad. Hold her every time she needs to be held and you will always be her best lover ever. It is as simple as that."*

— John Gottman, The Man's Guide to Women

I love this 'Hold her' paragraph for several reasons.

First, it encapsulates beautifully what a woman needs from her husband.

Second, all female clients to whom I have read this segment have approved and liked it.

Third, it holds truth which probably won't pass the test of 'political correctness' or radical feminism.

Fourth, it was written by John Gottman, the renowned marriage researcher and educator. Many practitioners like myself are heavily guided and inspired by his teaching, which can be traced in many pages of this book. When such an authority writes such a powerful paragraph, we should all listen.

But is it really *"as simple as that"*?

Gottman doesn't elaborate on how to "hold her." I guess ambiguity, in this case, helps him to avoid being blamed for 'masculine ideology.' But I won't leave it to you to guess. *The Good Husband* model will offer you specific tools to 'hold her' to keep your wife feeling secure and calm. These are primal feminine desires and it is essential that you fulfill them if you wish to make your wife happy.

As briefly mentioned at the end of Chapter Two, *The Good Husband* model is based on four masculine archetypes. Archetypes are psychological roles reflected in symbols, images, and patterns of thinking and behaving. Archetypes operate in our subconscious as universal blueprints inherited from our ancestors and common to all cultures. They exist as energy—as **potentials**—and they are manifested in the roles we take. This is why I use the words "role" and "energy" interchangeably.

The Ancient Greek word *arche* means "first principle" or "primal element." The four typical male roles originated in the male psyche many years ago. They tell the story of how evolutionary forces came to shape us over millions of years. We don't choose these ancient instincts, but we can choose how to utilize them to our advantage.

The four masculine roles

Four core archetypes—roles—define the mature male.

- KING,
- LOVER,
- MAGICIAN,
- WARRIOR.

To describe them, I take inspiration from the classic book *King, Warrior, Magician, Lover: Rediscovering the Archetypes of the Mature Masculine.*[41] Each of these roles represents the needs, strengths, and desires of mature and integral masculinity in men. These roles are expressed in ways of thinking, knowing, acting, and relating. They are your natural assets as a man. You want to treasure them, utilize them, and take pride in them. I have introduced these four roles to countless men, and the response is always positive. They are inspired by these images.

Why?

Because they represent sleeping potential deep in their psyche that is waiting to be awakened.

Each role has two poles:

1. the active pole (where it is expressed too strongly), and
2. the passive pole (where it is expressed too weakly).

These poles create a negative expression of the role, also known as the 'shadow.' Think of this shadow as a virus that corrupts an app. If it's not used wisely, any potential may harm rather than help. At the extreme poles, your asset of masculine energy becomes a liability; it can be used to harm yourself and others.

Aristotle said that virtue is found midway between the excess and the deficiency of a quality. (Did you know the word "virtue" has Latin roots that mean manliness?) Aristotle's philosophy of ethics has endured for two thousand five hundred years because it is practical and grounded in reality. He taught us that virtue is the art of balance. To serve you well and constructively, the role should be expressed in the middle of its active and passive pole. We find support for this idea in the book *T: The Story*

of Testosterone, the Hormone that Dominates and Divides Us.
The evolutionary biologist Dr. Carole Hooven explains how testosterone at its extremes can either be toxic or emasculating, but the proper expression of it leads to vigor and strength.[42]

To reach this balance, you need to cultivate self-awareness and watch out for any inflated or deflated expressions of the 'shadow.' Let's keep this in mind as we learn about the identity of each role.

Applying the four roles

You are about to learn how to access the male archetypes and power them up in your family life as your roles. The term "role" is not only user-friendly, but it also conveys the idea that you can swap hats and act in a different role when conditions require it. You act as a casting director who chooses the role most relevant to a situation in your family life. For example, you can say to yourself "This is the moment I need to act as a Warrior." You do not want to take roles too seriously. You are the director of your masculine roles!

Getting into a role is like playing a character; to play characters well, you need to understand how they think and feel. Once you know these four roles well, you can tap into them and use them as your resource. You will have an arsenal of characteristics to exhibit as a competent husband. Each role will equip you with a unique set of tools and strategies. When well balanced and applied in the right context, these roles will empower you to be the good husband you want to be.

I have arranged each role in a way that makes it easier for you to grasp its essence and understand its function. Think of these roles as apps on your smartphone. To operate them effectively, you need to know their functions well.

The King

Kings are our leaders, managers, captains, directors, and teachers. They lead, guide, and inspire us. The King is the central role (energy) which holds all other energies. Masculine traits which confirm and boost the King are:

- leadership,
- a sense of agency, being an instigator,
- vision, being intentional,
- being honorable,
- wisdom,
- holding up under pressure, and
- self-regulation.

Whether you like it or not, once you and your wife become parents you also become a King and a Queen. The question is only what kind of 'kingdom' you create for your children. Sitting on your 'throne' is a good start to fully embracing your role of authority in your child's life. It is a role that comes with immense responsibility and meaning.

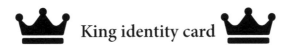

King identity card

My identity	I am the leader, the authority, the father, the manager, the person in charge.
My purpose	To lead and create order.
My questions	What is the most important thing here? What are my values? How to create order and security?
How I work	I provide direction and vision. I set values and rules. I make a difference in people's lives. I rule with love and respect, rather than through threats and force. I bless others.
My virtues	Leadership, integrity, centeredness, wisdom, contribution, balance, peace.
Embodiment	Sit upright, look straight, move gracefully and slowly. Consider your 'gravitas.' Having gravitas means that you matter to others. Your words speak volumes because you mean what you say. People high on gravitas can persuade and influence. They speak with intent, slowly, and quietly, and say little. Others listen.

Negative husband expressions of the King role

Over-active	Under-active	Dark side
obsessed with control and order	abdicates the 'throne'	tyrant
authoritarian	lets his wife lead alone	suspicious
condescending	lacks leadership or initiative	rules with fear
arrogant	reactive	paranoid
know-it-all	chaotic	
talks a lot		

Warning about the King

As you can imagine, using the concept of the King in the current anti-patriarchy and cultural bug climate can be risky. I learned this firsthand when the Family Court subpoenaed my clinical notes in a divorce case. The wife's lawyer read in the notes how I spoke to the husband about the King archetype. She argued to the judge that this concept illustrated patriarchy and a desire to control, which is not a desirable environment for a child. Luckily, the judge (a 'King' himself) laughed it off.

Unfortunately, taming by shaming works in some cases. Many men (including many men's movement groups) are too afraid of using the King concept themselves.

The irony is that talking to my female clients about the Queen archetype has been an integral part of their empowerment process for many years. They have always responded with enthusiasm to the concept! So, if you ever consider using this "King" term with your wife, make sure you always talk about the King **and** the Queen in the family.

The Lover

The Lover connects the other three masculine roles to life, people, and the vision that we are one—living, interconnected, and part of something larger than our ego or our tribe. The Lover is about what unites us rather than what separates us. Without Lover energy, a person is fragmented, detached, and even cruel at times. Lover energy reminds people of their true purpose and who they serve. That is why soccer players often walk onto the field holding children's hands before big matches. It reminds them of what truly matters in life beyond the desired sporting trophy or victory.

Lover energy is about being, love, and ultimately our happiness. Lovers are the artists, caregivers, visionaries, spiritual teachers, idealists, and of course, your family members and friends. Masculine traits linked to the Lover are:

- idealism,
- creativity,
- a sense of humor, and
- expression in your close relationships—desiring her, pursuing and leading the mating game, maintaining connection, and fathering your children.

Lover identity card

My identity	I am one with the world and with people. I am connected, I am in my body, I am now. I am spontaneous. I feel things, I am sensual.
My purpose	To connect with all, to love and share, to enjoy being, and to experience things fully.
My questions	What does she need? What do I need? What do we both feel? How can I make her feel good?
How I work	I enjoy the moment. I connect to people. I empathize. I worship beauty and indulge my senses. I dream. I know no boundaries.
My virtues	Kindness, caring, connectedness, joy, hope, enthusiasm, gratitude, and spirituality.
Embodiment	Hold a baby and sense what happens in your body. Enjoy family and friends, play, laugh, dance, savor the moment, walk in nature, make love, be part of a small group, meditate, pray.

Negative husband expressions of the Lover role

Over-active	Under-active	Dark side
immersed in ideals and fantasies	emotionally flattened	narcissist
restlessly indulges the senses	distant empty	addict
gets addicted	unmotivated	suicidal
poor boundaries	depressed	victim mentality
childish	his low energy drags his wife down	

The Magician

Magicians are people with the capacity to transform situations and influence both others and themselves. These are the scientists, researchers, philosophers, consultants, marketers, futurists, motivational speakers, and psychotherapists. Think of the wise sage, the shaman, and the guru. Buddha and Jesus.

During the coronavirus pandemic, when medical scientists helped leaders make decisions, we could watch closely how the relationships between Magicians and Kings work. You can recognize the Magician within yourself each time you self-soothe or try to talk yourself out of anger or worry. Masculine traits linked to the Magician are:

- stoic,
- clever, problem-solver,
- oriented to data and science,
- rational, and
- non-reactive.

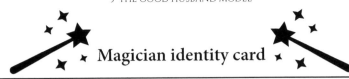

Magician identity card

My identity	I am the King's adviser. I am wise, I am self-aware, I am a clear mind.
My purpose	To transform, to invent, to research, to help the King make good decisions, to bring clarity in times of chaos.
My questions	What is happening here? What do I need to understand and see? How to transform this situation? Does it work?
How I work	I use my mind to see processes at a deeper level. I examine. I consult. I regulate emotions to keep a clear mind. I invent things. I change situations. I influence people. I act as a 'bullshit detector'—I see through denial and exercise discernment.
My virtues	Perspective, non-reactiveness, curiosity, mindfulness, self-awareness, learning, insight, critical thinking, deep understanding of processes, objective observations.
Embodiment	Calm, grounded presence, alertness of senses—observe, see, hear. Mindfulness—focused and clear mind to see reality for what it is. Respond with "I hear you…" or "I see you…"

Negative husband expressions of the Magician role

Over-active	Under-active	Dark side
emotionally detached problem-focused	confused	cult leader
too cerebral	fuzzy	manipulator
lost in thought	resigned	conman
(confession: this is an area my family has complained to me about...)	overwhelmed	charlatan
	indecisive	(recall how the snake hypnotized Mowgli in *The Jungle Book* movie.)
	unconscious	
	denying	

The Warrior

Warriors are the people who work hard to achieve their goals, protect their boundaries, and fight for values such as justice and freedom. These are our soldiers, first responders, politicians, reporters, lawyers, businessmen, advocates, elite sportsmen, and hard-working men. Masculine traits which confirm and boost the Warrior are:

- strength,
- courage,
- goal orientation,
- assertiveness, and
- risk-taking.

Each time you take on a challenge, you activate your Warrior.

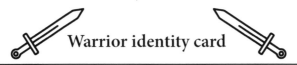

Warrior identity card

My identity	I am a doer, a go-getter, a man of action, a fighter, a protector, and a problem-fixer, and I work hard to achieve my goals.
My purpose	To accomplish goals, to succeed on missions, to fight for values such as family, nation, justice, freedom, or my faith.
My questions	What do I need to do here? How can I help? What is the challenge? What is the solution?
How I work	I act. I take on challenges. I solve problems. I confront issues. I assert boundaries.
My virtues	Courage, resilience, action orientation, decision-making, endurance, loyalty, focus, discipline, commitment.
Embodiment	Imagine your child or wife is in danger. What you feel in your body is the energy of the Warrior—ready to act, focused, determined, and clear about what you are supposed to do.

Negative husband expressions of the Warrior role

Over-active	Under-active	Dark side
workaholic	passive	bully
risky behaviors	avoids conflicts	ruthless
suppressed vulnerability	the 'nice guy'	cruel
thinks in black and white	lazy	corrupt
perfectionist	neglects self	
with family, he might be combative, aggressive, and lack empathy.	undisciplined	
	unmotivated	
	weak	

Illustration of the four masculine roles in action

Let's take a simple scenario from family life to illustrate how we utilize these four roles. Imagine your wife is angry with your son and she blames you for not doing enough to help her control him.

As a King, you operate according to the values and rules of your family. You discuss the rules and consequences, and you seek consistency in how you and your wife apply them. You explain to your children the values behind your rules (for example, kindness, respect, and honesty). You seek to collaborate and align with your partner on your discipline principles.

As a Lover, you focus on your wife's feelings and needs. You listen, relate to her frustration, get closer to help her calm down, and you offer support.

As a Magician, you don't react but try to understand and solve the problem. You sense the discomfort of being blamed, but you don't react with defensiveness or counter blame your wife. You don't take things personally but instead notice what is happening and try to make sense of the situation. You ask questions in an attempt to better understand and solve the problem.

As a Warrior, you take action and set boundaries. You tell your son that you expect him to show respect to his mother and help her enforce consequences.

YOUR STRENGTHS AND HER VULNERABILITIES

Your wife needs your strengths in the area where she feels most vulnerable—her need to feel safe and secure. Cross-cultural research shows that women are prone to experience anxiety in far greater numbers than men.[43,44,45] In her book *The Female Brain*, Louann Brizendine explains how unique brain mechanisms make women far more prone to depression and anxiety than men.[46] If our testosterone makes us more aggressive, her hormones make her more moody and anxious.

In seeking security, her psyche listens to the wisdom of evolution.

- First, her body is the desired object for many men; sadly, some are dangerous.

- Second, her body carries the collective memory of trauma and brutality at the hands of men throughout the history of mankind, including abuse, rape, sexual exploitation, and burning.

- Third, she needs to cope with internal threats as well—those constant fluctuations in the levels of chemistry and hormones in her body. These fluctuations are particularly intense during the time of raising babies.

- Fourth, mother nature allocated to her the very risky, demanding, and precious mission of producing and maintaining life. She bears the responsibility of caring for a fragile newborn baby, a highly daunting task that makes women feel vulnerable. Over the centuries, women have also lost their lives during childbirth.

When affected by anxiety, people tend to ruminate and get lost in their thinking and their stories. If you deeply understand the huge place that anxiety has in your wife's psyche, then you will realize how trust is so crucial and fragile in your relationship. You will avoid behaviors that may damage this trust. And you will also take her attitude and behaviors less personally. So much of her worries, anger, and complaints have nothing to do with you even when they sound like they do!

Nevertheless, you have a great deal of power in healing her pain. This is the message of the 'Hold her' opening paragraph of this chapter.

The 'sensitivity to safety' issue is so big for women that people affected by the cultural bug manipulate and exploit it frequently by using the code name "unsafe." This word has become a precursor for limiting others' free expression to avoid 'hurting feelings.'

Let's take a closer look at how each of the masculine roles can enable you to help your wife with her feminine vulnerabilities.

Her need for emotional security

Anxiety is highly prevalent among women worldwide, but interestingly, women in Western countries are even more anxious than their sisters in more traditional cultures.[47] Australia, for example, is one of the safest places on earth, yet, anxiety is the number one mental health issue.[48,49]

Why?

Because in Western countries, personal liberties and individualism are valued so highly that they come at the expense of communal values which keep us closer to one another, such as marriage, family, and community. Communities with less connectedness and social structure are less conducive to providing the social order and security that women crave. This need for security is even more burning when you raise young kids. Mothers identify with the vulnerability of their children and mirror their need for security, belonging, and structure.

You can use your King energy to provide her with order, stability, and security.

Her need to feel desired

Your wife's identification with her body is similar to how you identify with your career. After all, it is her body that gives her the ultimate power to attract the right man for her reproductive mission. When she is wanted and touched, her sense of self-worth grows. Changes in her body may damage this worth and constantly challenge her self-image.

Sociologist Catherine Hakim suggests that the female body and attractiveness are 'erotic capital' for a woman—her unique assets to be used as part of her power.[50] When you desire her, you validate her unique power. She gets a boost to her self-worth. If she doesn't feel desired by you, mistrust and fears of rejection may secretly grow in the back of her mind.

Singer Beverley Craven sings, "I am just an old-fashioned girl who wants you to make a move on me. So why can't you just be the man." It is not 'old-fashioned,' but her ancient feminine instincts.

You can use your Lover energy to connect, show affection, and show her she is wanted.

Her need for clarity

As a woman, she is tuned to her body and affected by it. Her feelings and motherly instincts often serve her as guides. Her top qualities as a mother are being sensitive and responsive to her babies every time they make a sound. She is naturally highly reactive.

Further, regular changes in her body (such as hormonal changes) affect her moods and feelings. These changes may affect her judgment and her desires. They may result in blurry thinking, indecisiveness, and heavy self-doubts about herself, her motherhood, or her choices.

You can use your Magician energy to bring more clarity and objectivity to help her keep things in perspective.

Her need to feel protected

Can you think of the last time you were afraid for your life? This fear can be a daily event for a woman. I see that during my night walks when occasionally a woman crosses to the other side of the street to avoid me. A woman is innately anxious about all kinds of safety matters and for a good reason. Females are more vulnerable to attacks.

If you raise a daughter, you should have an inkling of this. It's scary. Fathers can relate to that sense of protectiveness. Women also tend to be more agreeable than men, so they often fail to set clear boundaries for others, particularly those outside their immediate family.[51]

You can use your Warrior energy to set boundaries around your family, protect and keep your wife safe, and elicit her respect and trust.

The masculine roles and your dysfunctional patterns

There are a few dysfunctional patterns that men commonly bring into their relationships. These patterns compromise men's constructive power and damage their marriages. Let's recognize them and reflect on what energy you can tap into to get back to your center if you have any of these dysfunctional patterns.

The nice guy

In his book *No More Mr. Nice Guy*, Dr. Robert Glover describes how this dysfunctional style makes a man lose power. This man avoids conflicts and tries hard to please others. He believes that if he is nice, giving, and caring, he will be liked and get what he wants.[52] However, because he fears rejection and avoids confrontation, he is not assertive enough in situations where he should be, and consequently things don't go his way.

When Mr. Nice Guy becomes frustrated, he may act in a passive-aggressive way. His avoidance only makes matters worse. Issues don't get resolved and his wife gets increasingly angry. Further, his avoidance of conflicts means that she cannot trust him to stand up for her and the interests of the family.

If this is you, activate your Warrior energy to get things done, assert your boundaries, and confront issues with courage.

The workaholic guy

The workaholic man regards his career, success, and money as more important than his relationship with his family. As much as he is an excellent provider, he doesn't meet his wife's needs for connection and support. Too often, this workaholic lifestyle also comes at the expense of his relationship with his kids.

His wife feels secure financially but lonely emotionally. This need for connection can be particularly crucial in our modern culture where partners rely heavily on each other for social and emotional needs. Women in such relationships often feel less of a priority for him, deserted, lonely, and sad.

If this is you, activate your Lover energy to balance work with family life and leisure time.

The immature guy

The immature guy is driven by a core need for closeness and security. This need expresses itself as high levels of dependency and a deep fear of separation. His need for attachment will drive him to demand attention and regular connection. Such a man was likely brought up by an over-protective mother and a weak or absent father. He lacked challenges and clear boundaries.

Now he expects his wife to meet his emotional needs, just like his mother. This might seem charming initially, and for certain women, it may offer a sense of power. Yet, once children arrive, her expectations change. Anger and disdain are likely to replace her motherly support.

If this is you, activate your Warrior energy to help you pursue your independence and achieve your goals.

The logical guy

Highly passionate about his beliefs and opinions, this man may try to convince his wife with logic and reasoning about what should be 'the right way.' He is like a lawyer in disguise. Alas, his arguments don't impress her; they exhaust her instead. She seeks understanding of her feelings and needs rather than logical arguments.

This mismatch creates a frustrating gridlock where issues are not resolved on a deeper, emotional level. He feels powerless because his smart words have no impact, and she becomes frustrated that her man doesn't 'get' her.

If this is you, activate your Magician energy to gain insights into your fruitless patterns and find effective ways to touch and influence her.

The controlling guy

In my clinical observations, the classical controlling man is far less common these days. However, the area where men do try to exercise control is money. It is still more common to see the man as the primary breadwinner; as such, he feels more in charge over this area of family life. When the man sets tight restrictions on spending out of anxiety, his partner feels a loss of freedom and a lack of respect. The result is growing resentment and distance.

If this is you, activate your Lover and your wise King.

The impulsive-addictive guy

With impulse control issues, this man is more prone to chaotic or addictive habits, such as alcohol, drugs, and porn—a highly distressing and very common concern for women. These chaotic patterns distract the man from his responsibilities.

His wife feels edgy and vigilant. His unpredictable or addictive behaviors make it hard to rely on him. This man gradually loses her respect and her trust.

If this is you, activate your King and Magician energies.

Your power redefined

Now that you understand the potential in your masculine roles, we can describe your power as **how effectively you exhibit your masculine roles to make a positive difference in your family.** Power doesn't mean having an immediate impact. Regardless of how well you use these navigation tools, you cannot control your wife, and often you may barely be able to understand her.

Don't get discouraged if capitalizing on your strengths doesn't bring you instant results. After all, this relationship guide is for **ways** of *being*, **ways** *of doing, and* **ways** *of relating* in your family. Your constructive power is not measured in terms of instant outcomes but in terms of **how** you do things. Not controlling, but influencing. Your wife takes notice even when you can't see the immediate impact.

To be wise is to ask what works and what influences. Research on long-term marriages tells us that partners do not solve more than two-thirds of their problems![53] Yet, they are still together.

Why?

Because they wisely focus their energy on the one-third of problems that they can manage, while learning to accommodate, compromise, and accept the other two-thirds that they cannot change. Now that you are equipped with *The Good Husband* navigation tools, let's head out to the ocean and practice some sailing!

PART TWO

THE PRACTICE

In order to make the best use of the tools and strategies you are about to learn, I suggest you keep the following principles in mind.

Practice principles

Clarity is energizing

Each of the four roles in *The Good Husband* model offers you a clear path to express your masculine strengths. Role clarity refers to perceptions, beliefs, and expectations about how you are supposed to behave. Confusion is paralyzing, while role clarity is energizing and gives confidence to act.

Clarity gives you the confidence and reassurance that you are doing the right thing. Role clarity leads you to behave in a certain way. This book has done its job if it helps you to gain clarity of the good qualities in your masculine identity, so that you fit comfortably into your masculine role in your family.

Acceptance before change

The paradox of change is that to change our thinking and feelings, we first need to accept them. Accept rather than judge; accept rather than resist or fight. What helps us to accept is understanding the complexity of an issue. Understanding and accepting weaknesses and unpleasant experiences (e.g. fears, conflicts) means to regard them as the reality you need to manage. It is what it is. Acceptance is the opposite of denial, avoidance, or resistance.

A hallmark of deep understanding and true acceptance of an unpleasant experience is that we feel sad rather than angry. Sadness is a noble and healthy emotion. It enables letting go, moving on, and investing energy in the areas where we can make a difference. This is wisdom.

Practice makes progress

The greatest ideas and insights are useless if they are not applied. Practicing your masculine strengths will enable you to cultivate and grow them until you achieve a sense of mastery. Before mastering any skill, you must be willing to try, fail, and then try again. Since we are talking about life skills in this book, your practice is a life journey. It's a process that never ends. After all, we are talking about important values that you can express through your masculine strengths.

Most segments in this book conclude with some practices for you to follow. They are easy to implement and usually done in collaboration with your partner. If you wish to evolve rather than revolve, you will have to put in the effort.

Ideas to inspire and motivate

Sometimes the roles may sound like they have impossibly high standards to meet. Use them as a source of guidance and inspiration, rather than a benchmark you must attain to be a good husband. There is already enough pressure on you to perform. Focus on what works, avoid judging your vulnerabilities, and keep self-acceptance high in your consciousness. Rather than dealing with more shame, we want you to feel supported and strengthened!

Go gently. It is tempting to take the model as some kind of recipe to become the perfect husband. That might be her dream, but not yours. Higher standards mean higher expectations and more judgment, which may result in more shame for your poor performance. Make sure this model is not serving as yet another avenue to shame you.

A healthy approach can be to focus your attention and intention on a single growth area at a time. Further, it's important to understand that certain solutions may not always perfectly suit your unique circumstances and personality. Instead, try to follow the spirit and logic of how each role operates.

4

ACTIVATE YOUR KING TO CREATE ORDER

"The King's first responsibility is to live according to The Way. If he does, everything in the kingdom will also go according to the Right Order. The kingdom will flourish."

— Robert Moore and Douglas Gillette, King, Warrior, Magician, Lover

We start by activating your role as a King in your family because this capability will direct all your other roles (Lover, Magician, and Warrior). Here is a brief reminder of the King identity card that I described in more detail in Chapter Three:

My identity	I am the leader, the authority, the father, the manager.
My purpose	To lead and to create order.
How I work	I provide direction and vision. I set values and rules. I am intentional.

Her voice:

"As a mother, I feel in my body nearly everything our kids experience. I feel their pain, I feel their joy. They are like a part of me. I am as vulnerable as they are, as sad as they are, and as happy as they are. You will never understand the intensity of this experience. It is not that I have become some kind of moody and unpredictable person. I get emotional and distressed for a reason. I echo their experiences when they are anxious, needy, demanding, and unpredictable.

Their demand for my attention can feel overwhelming. You may ignore their crying, but I feel compelled to respond. Their chaos may become my own internal chaos. Fog, self-doubts, and confusion can overtake me. When I am not able to stop their pain, I feel lost, powerless, and inadequate. To help me in such moments of turmoil, I need you to remain centered and make sure our life is in order. I need you to support me by taking the lead to ensure a stable and safe environment for us. This will make me feel secure and calm."

A King is an agent of growth and building. His crown is a symbol of authority. He authors the future with the power of his words. He is intentional. He leads with a vision—a vision for the nation, the organization, and the family. To keep the vision alive, a King creates an order. This is a set of values, laws, principles, and rules. It is 'the way.' The way is not about goals and strategies but about **how** we live moment by moment. Goals may change, but a King's values and principles remain the backbone that holds his family upright. Kings fully understand the danger of chaos, and the importance of order for successful functioning. This order will guarantee that "The kingdom will flourish."

For a King, the responsibility always stops with him. He takes charge of situations, and he focuses on getting back to the 'right order'—the way. When problems occur, he blames no one, focusing his energy on finding solutions instead. He doesn't play the victim or oppose anyone. He is too busy maintaining order and leading towards a better future. In that sense, a King is 'positive.' He is **for** something, rather than against.

Confident in his way (the 'right order'), a King is not easily overwhelmed or swayed. As the center for the other three energies (Lover, Magician, and Warrior), he integrates good principles and leads with integrity, clarity, and focus, even during times of stress or crisis.

A King represents abundance. He has reached a place where he doesn't need to own more than he already has. He has no sense of scarcity, so he can focus on serving and protecting others—his family, community, and nation. He gives blessing, encouragement, and inspiration to others.

The King of your family

Whether you like it or not, you and your wife both become a King and a Queen the moment your child is born. Being a father means playing the role of a King. Your child will look up to you as a source of security, guidance, and inspiration. It is your choice as to what kind of King you want to be. If you are too rigid and controlling, you will come across as a tyrant and provoke fear and resistance. If you are too soft, then your words will not be respected, and you won't be able to provide the security your family needs from you.

Most men love their identity as a father (a King) for their children. They embrace it with enthusiasm and love to act on it. There is no risk to you if you are not a good father. This is different from your role as a husband, which is far more complex and relates to Kings' relationships with their Queens. So let's spend a moment understanding your partner.

Your wife might be a successful and competent professional, but when it comes to her children, mother nature speaks louder than any trendy social norms. She literally feels your child's moods and is compelled to react. Her reactivity is not that different from how our male bodies react to seeing sexy women or sexual stimuli.

When my daughter was six months old and crying heavily, I tried to comfort her. My wife came out of the bathroom, and I noticed her breasts were leaking milk. I realized the big difference between my reaction and her reaction. For me, my daughter's crying was a problem to solve, but for her, it was an experience that involved her entire body. A child's pain is a mother's pain.

After giving birth, feminine energy is expressed in its full glory: care, empathy, sensitivity, attunement, responsiveness, and devotion. Motherhood is a gift that nature has bestowed upon women over the course of millions of years of evolution. But this gift came at a price.

Female identification with the experiences of their kids is biologically driven and it can be challenging when dealing with young, chaotic children who are impulsive, emotional, anxious, and unpredictable. Since the motherly instinct is designed to make women responsive to their children, their children's chaos rubs off on them. So, your partner's parenting experience often intensifies her feelings of vulnerability, dependency, anxiety, and at times inadequacies and powerlessness. The emotional rollercoaster of motherhood can be debilitating.

It is essential that you understand the impact of parenting on your wife's psyche. Only then can you meet her need for the right type of support from you. When she is vulnerable and emotional, she needs you to stay calm and centered. When she is dependent, she needs you to be dependable. For your "kingdom to flourish," both she and your children need you to take the lead and create order as the King of your family.

If motherhood is her gift from nature, the ability to create order is your gift via your masculine energy. Yet, unlike the motherhood instinct, which is expressed through dramatic changes in her female physiology, such as breastfeeding, your King energy requires your conscious intention and effort for it to emerge. This is one of the significant differences between men and women.

Feminine chaos and masculine order

Chaos (the unknown) is symbolically associated with feminine energy. Motherhood, nature, and chaos represent the sources from which life emerges. As in nature, the feminine follows a bottom-up process. It emerges effortlessly and spontaneously, yet n without a clear direction or order. This is also true of the motherhood instinct.

Men, by comparison, tend to follow top-down processes. We complement mothers by creating order (the known) from chaos (the unknown). While being feminine is about being natural, being masculine is about being conscious and intentional; it requires some practice before our masculine gifts are honed.

Our masculine responsibilities require our intention and will. We need to master nature, regulate our bodies, envisage possibilities, and design the future. This is the meaning of the King's crown. It stresses the importance of the head and its executive functioning—having a vision, planning ahead, leading, organizing, strategizing, self-regulating, and committing. These values might be treated with cynicism or suspicion (for example, as "patriarchy") among some groups, but you should not be discouraged by that. There is no reason ever to abdicate your King's throne. Being a King is your responsibility as a man, not an entitlement. Similarly, being a Queen is the responsibility of your wife.

The King's word

Using and understanding language are unique human capacities. Language enables us to master both our internal and external environments. Using language to express what we want or need is a hallmark of maturity. Kings use language to make a difference at the group level. They use the power of their words to create and manage social order in their families, organizations, and nations. This social order determines how successful social structures are.

The origin of the word 'spell' means 'to tell.' With the magical power of words, you can enchant people—'put a spell' on them. Consider for a moment the words—'yes' and 'no.' 'No' is energetically associated with danger. It is the language of survival instincts. When we are reactive, we mostly default to avoidance or resistance. If your children and wife are insecure, this will be their default mindset. To lead, you have to use the power of 'yes.' Your intentional and constructive language then creates possibilities, and your 'yes' words guide and inspire about the Way—the kind of norms and standards you want to create in your family.

The story of Genesis in the old scripture illustrates this power: "*And God said, Let there be light: and there was light.*" Our ancestors were wise enough to acknowledge this unique power as human beings, hence why they wrote that we were created "in the image of God." Interestingly, we cannot be sure about the presence of God, but we can be sure that the concept of God is being created in our mind through our language. With this power of the word, we can also design our future and rule both nature and our bodies. For example, to regulate emotions, we label them.

Your words carry weight. But what determines this weight? What makes people treat your words seriously? This will depend on your own relationship with your words. If you 'walk the talk,' then people will trust and rely on what you say. They will know that you expect them to take your words seriously. You speak slowly, with few words, clearly showing that every word you say matters. You mean what you say. When you speak with your authority, you expect people to listen because your words are aimed at serving them, not your ego. You lead and provide security.

As a King, your might is not in your sword but in your word.

What do we mean by 'order'?

Order refers to a set of 'statements' by which people live. These statements can take the form of a vision, a mission statement, declarations, laws, rules, vows, guidelines, protocols, frameworks, and so on. The most famous statements that establish order in the Judeo-Christian tradition are *The Ten Commandments*.

On the interpersonal level, order statements will take the form of agreements, contracts, vows, commitments, and promises. On the personal level, we talk about values, goals, and plans.

As you can see, order begins with words. When you act on your words, you lead. Your words express 'your way', and your actions fulfill it. When your actions match your words, we call it integrity. Giving and keeping your word is how you express your honor and your integrity.

However, if you have a loose relationship with your words, then you create a situation where people stop taking you seriously. Your authority is compromised, and when this happens, your 'kingdom' gets weaker. Your children need order from you to facilitate their growth from chaotic infants into mature and orderly adults.

"The King's energy helps me do what matters, no matter what."

— **Anonymous**

Why order?

In free nations, parliament is the heart of democracy. What is the most common word you may hear there? Order. To guarantee healthy and effective processes in any organization, we must have order.

Order is a hallmark of flourishing nations, successful companies, and highly functional families. Think of the most complex systems, such as governments, armies, justice systems, airports, and hospitals. To function successfully, they must create order. Order creates system security and reliability. When rules are applied consistently across the board, it also creates a sense of fairness. People feel they can trust the system.

Research on judgment and decision-making shows that when leaders do not follow an orderly and systematic process of decision-making, they risk "noise."[54] Noise is the large variability of solutions and outcomes for the same problem. It creates a lack of consistency and leads to the loss of credibility. Noise happens when professionals in positions of power offer very different solutions to the same problem (for example, very different punishments for the same crime). The judgment is based on subjective experiences such as intuition, impression, prejudice, and mood. The wise King, on the other hand, will base his judgment and decisions on clear principles.

Here are some good reasons for you to create order in your family:

- **Order creates security.**
  This means more certainty, predictability, and stability for your family.

- **Order creates trust.**

  This means your family can rely on you and each other.
  You can all expect and predict how everyone will behave.

- **Order creates rationality.**

  When things make sense, you can reason with one another
  and seek reasonable solutions to problems.

- **Order creates fairness.**

  The rules or agreements are applied equally and
  consistently.

- **Order creates a sense of mastery and efficacy.**

  This makes the operation of running a household effective
  and efficient. This is why order leads to the success of
  nations, firms, and families.

- **Order creates a sense of personal power.**

  When things run smoothly, people feel competent and
  confident, with immense impact on motivation and
  productivity.

- **Order creates inner peace.**

  When we remain loyal to our values and principles, we
  save ourselves from battling demons such as anxiety, guilt,
  regret, and shame. Commitment to your own truth (to
  your crown) will guarantee peace in your heart.

- **Order is wise and a source of more wisdom.**

  When people try to assess, judge, or predict based on
  feeling, intuition, and impression, they risk making
  judgment errors. Instead, the wise King follows an orderly
  process based on what leads to the best outcomes. His way
  is anchored in a deep understanding of human nature.
  In the world of the wise King, ideals meet reality. He is
  anchored deep in the ground with his head high in the sky.

Let's think for a moment about the opposite of order—chaos.

Chaos in the family is characterized by disorganization, confusion, and poor discipline practices. Among chaotic families, more children suffer from ADHD, socio-emotional issues, and poorer academic performance. Chaos will also result in more family conflicts, a sense of failure, parental dissatisfaction, and health issues.

If parental authority is vague or absent, the vacuum will be filled by the 'gremlins' of the mind: assumptions, interpretations, and suspicions. A home environment without authority breeds anxiety. Families without order become increasingly dysfunctional and experience more blaming and shaming. You may have even experienced it yourself growing up. I did.

However, when you serve as a model of order in your behavior, live by your values and principles, mean what you say, and are predictable in your actions, your family can feel safe and calm. Your children will grow to feel secure.

Consider your family your 'kingdom' and give them order to help them flourish. This is your ultimate expression of leadership.

Challenges to creating order

You may not always feel at ease in your King role of authority. After all, you may have rebelled against authority when you were younger, preferring the charm, spontaneity, and fun that comes with being free-spirited instead. Acting on your boyish energy may feel more tempting regarding leisure, drugs, alcohol, or other sensual activities. Activating your King role may take some adjustment and willpower.

For your partner, the challenge to assuming your King role is the perception of hierarchy. Women seek equality, fairness, and sharing, while a hierarchy is associated with an imbalance of power. At times, she may perceive that your creating order is an attempt at controlling, which may encourage her to align more with your kids than with you as an authority figure. This is a very common challenge for men. While disciplining a child, their wives interfere to 'protect' the child from them. (We will discuss parenting issues in Chapter Nine).

And there is the cultural challenge of creating order. We live in an open society with instant access to an endless source of information and ideas. This can be overwhelming and confusing. Openness and inclusiveness towards various kinds of lifestyles are highly celebrated values. Order sounds like an old-fashioned concept associated with traditional lifestyles or controlling behaviors. However, when you raise a family, your children and their needs will set the tone. Creating order for them is paramount because it goes straight to their basic need for security.

THE KING IN ACTION

These are the tools you will need to activate your inner King:

- developing and maintaining family values,
- ensuring accountability,
- developing and enforcing family rules,
- clarifying family roles and tasks,
- managing financial matters in an orderly manner,
- creating rituals, and
- accepting influence.

Let's look at each tool in more detail.

Develop and maintain family values

Values are your inner guides. They stem from your heart's deepest desires. For example, kindness, loyalty, care, honesty, respect, hope, courage, gratitude, and perseverance. Values serve as your compass while you are sailing on the ocean of life. Your deeply held values will reflect what matters the most to you, the kind of person you want to be, and the kind of family you wish to raise.

To know your values, you only need to look at your behavior patterns: how you interact with others and how you spend your psychic energy, time, and money. Ultimately, your actions tell the story of who you are, while your words suggest who you want to be.

Answer these questions:

- How much do my lifestyle and behavior reflect what is important to me?
- How close to my values do I live?

Most people operate on autopilot while navigating internal and external pressures in their lives. They don't lead. But when you have an organization, a company, or a family to run, you must sit on your King 'throne' and lead with your values. Instead of reacting to pressures with fleeting impulses or emotions, your responses are guided by your family values and rules that you and your Queen ideally agree on.

When you lead a values-driven life, you are more likely to experience your strength and be centered. You cannot always control the outcomes of living based on your values, but you can control how you act on them in the here and now!

Acting on your values will make you feel centered and more in charge of your life.

Outwardly, it will convey your reliability and strength. Inwardly, staying close to your values will also make you feel more at peace within yourself. Leading with your values will reduce the voice of your inner critic and its negative impacts—self-doubt, guilt, and shame. And as you learn to lead a values-driven family life, you are far more likely to make your family secure and happy.

To manifest your King energy in your family, your very first task is to be the '**Head of Values**' in your family. That doesn't mean you dictate what the family values are to your wife, but rather, you are the one who keeps **talking** about values. You bring the family back to "The Way" each time they lost the way. This is how you affect the top-down process—you keep your family aware of the values. You invest your intention and attention energies into the values that really matter in keeping your family happy, whether they be honesty, kindness, consideration, respect, or any other value. You lead by keeping the family vision alive.

Here are four good reasons for you to take on this values aspect of your King role:

1. When you instigate a conversation about a value, you also consolidate your own clarity and commitment to it. This helps keep you on track, so you don't get lost in the confusing 'forest' of your family life.

2. If you don't, you and your partner risk falling into a very common, reactive, and dangerous pattern in which you are both heavily invested in the short-term survival

tasks of parenting and breadwinning, while neglecting what matters so much for the long-term survival of your family—your connection. You will soon begin losing each other.

3. Without the positive focus on family values that you and your wife both want, your attention is diverted by what goes wrong, and you find yourselves being mostly reactive. Negative emotions, arguments, and complaints are often the results. With values you bring the power of Yes that I mentioned above.

4. Being reactive and responsive is how women naturally tend to operate at home. You hear it in the common use of oppositional language such as "no," "stop," and "don't." It reflects their vulnerability. You will help them by evoking positive intentions and values in your family life.

What to value

All of your family values matter a great deal, but you will be more effective in your King role if you focus your intention and attention on the particular value that helps you address each specific situation at a time.

Let's begin with the general challenge of losing connection with your partner over time, especially when raising a family. This is common to all couples. We all go through a phase when we lose connection, either emotionally or physically. Luckily, we can now rely on research to guide us on the kind of values that help us in this situation.

Couples who have stayed together over many years tell us that what helped them survive the turmoil of raising a family and sustain a meaningful connection was nourishing their

friendship. Friendship reflects important values such as loyalty, care, generosity, and consideration that build trust. You and your partner should regard each other as best friends. Imagine for a moment how your wife would respond if you made statements such as these:

- "I want us to get back to the friendship we used to have."
- "Let's do something to restore our friendship."
- "I miss our friendship."
- "I would like you to see me as your best friend."

As you can sense, talking about your friendship stimulates constructive dynamics in the relationship. It's like putting a train on a track. It is the power of positive conversation. Such a conversation is not a lofty dream. It is pretty much going back to basics. It only requires the attitudes and values you show towards your close friends.

Another important value to consider is **kindness.** Family members sometimes argue and fight. This is natural. But maintaining kindness during any conflicts is both crucial and a major challenge. It's so crucial that I sometimes describe my job as a 'kindness coach,' not a couples therapist. Couples I work with are well aware that my tolerance for any form of aggression is zero.

I encourage you to adopt a similar stance. If your family members don't treat each other with kindness, you may want to lead a conversation about it and consider ways to improve the kindness in your household. Imagine using dinner as an opportunity for parents and kids to share experiences of kindness from the day or week. Can you sense the positive impact on everyone?

A scarcity mindset is a common problem in many families. Children are notoriously ungrateful. The more they get what they want, the less tolerant they become toward not getting what they want. They end up taking you both for granted. Their continuous complaining may affect your wife and fill her with self-doubt about whether she is a good enough parent. If it does, it will soon affect your relationship. The antidote to a scarcity mindset is an abundance mindset. To cultivate an abundance mindset, you can introduce gratitude practice and integrate the habit of sharing gratitude into your family culture.

PRACTICE:

Initiate a conversation with your wife about values. Together, select two values and explain what makes these values so important to you and why. Discuss ways you both plan to act on each one. Here is a sample of some relationship values to choose from:

- kindness
- support
- friendship
- honesty
- fairness
- connection
- respect
- reliability
- self-discipline
- responsibility
- gratitude
- resilience

Create and enforce family rules

In your role as an authority figure in your family, both you and your wife need to set some rules for your children. These rules will serve a similar purpose to laws in society. Without boundaries and consequences, your family cannot function properly.

Even though the importance of rules is beyond question, too often parents are confused about what their rules are. Arguing about rules and enforcing them is a major source of marital conflicts.

Creating order and clarity in this area of childrearing is a matter of urgency for many relationships. Without rule clarity, your authority is less effective and your children feel less secure. Ineffective parenting leads to confusion and conflicts; family life then begins to spiral downwards.

How do you agree on the right rules to create order in your parenting?

Over the years, I have worked with a few ultra-Orthodox Jewish families. I have noticed an interesting phenomenon in some of these families. While family life during the week was complete chaos for them, it was the complete opposite on Saturdays, the Jewish holy day of the week. Everyone was calm and centered. Why? Because this was when the rules were very clear to the parents.

In the case of religion, the source of the rules stems from a perceived higher authority. But if you don't practice a religion, you may wonder how to choose your rules. What kind of moral authority should you rely on? What is really important? How flexible or rigid should you be?

Too much openness and flexibility may breed chaos and confusion. On the other hand, too much rigid authority and control may breed resentment and resistance. So, what is the right parenting approach?

When we look at elements of control and warmth in parenting styles, we see four different models. In an authoritarian model, control is too high and warmth is too low. In an indulgent model, warmth is too high and control is too low. In an uninvolved model, both control and warmth are low.

The ideal environment for children is the **authoritative** model where parents combine responsiveness with demands and challenges. They balance warmth with control. Children who grow up with the authoritative parenting style show the best developmental outcomes. They perform better in school and show better emotional and social adjustment. This parenting style creates a healthy balance between feminine and masculine strengths.

To achieve such a balance, it is crucial to sustain a healthy relationship between you and your wife. In a troubled relationship, you will often see a pattern where mothers blame fathers for being too rigid, and fathers blame mothers for being too soft.

Whatever rules and routine you both choose for your family life, the main challenge you face is enforcing those rules. This is where you need to tap into the wisdom quality that is part of your King energy. Being wise means considering the various factors at play when a rule is broken and showing some flexibility, rather than just rigidly enforcing rules.

As mentioned earlier, a mother identifies with the suffering of her child, internalizing it in her own body. This makes it harder for her to enforce consequences, which is why sleep schools for babies are effective: they separate the mother from the baby so she can't hear the crying. The younger the child, the harder it is for a mother. Your main contribution here is to understand your partner's vulnerability and not blame her for being too lenient or 'weak'. Only with true understanding will you be able to accept and support her, rather than be frustrated with her. Your frustration only further disempowers her and worsens any feelings of guilt and self-doubt that she may have.

I can't tell you how many times I have heard from a man that when his partner is away, their children are far better behaved. Naturally, a mother does not like to hear that because it sounds like proof of her failure. It isn't. It reflects the deep emotional attachment between children and their mothers. If you blame your partner for being too lenient or weak, or blame your child for being manipulative, then you are showing poor understanding of the complex emotions at play.

Wherever possible, use words of validation and empathy instead. For example:

- "Yeah, I know it's tough for you."
- "I see how her crying upset you."
- "Sorry you are so upset by it."

Yes, I am aware that it's not natural for many men to express themselves this way. But you will be amazed at how validating your wife's feelings and empathizing with them works so well.

Your understanding of her vulnerability can be stretched if she tries to stop you from being too strict on your child. She may judge you as being cruel. This is very common. It may even deteriorate to what is known as the 'Drama Triangle', in which your wife adopts the role of the rescuer, the child takes the role of the victim, and you are given the role of the perpetrator, the 'bad cop.' "They will hate you when they grow up!" said one mother to her husband when he banned TV for 3 days.

This Drama Triangle is a serious red flag. I elaborate further on how to manage it in the chapter on Fatherhood.

So, how can you maintain family rules and avoid escalating conflicts with your partner?

The best times to have a reasonable discussion about what is best for your child/children are when you both feel emotionally close and connected. The less connected you are, the more division you may experience over the good cop/bad cop issue. The wise thing to do is to invest in friendship and closeness with your wife. (More on the Lover role in the next chapter.)

But if you can't come to a reasonable agreement, and you believe that your wife's protectiveness is damaging both herself and your children, then I recommend you bring in a third party to help you both reflect on the situation. Your wife's natural vulnerability may stop her from admitting that her actions are bad for your children. She may argue strongly, leading you to struggle with reaching a reasonable solution. To get out of this cycle of arguments, consider involving outside people. Doctors and counselors can help, or any influential person who can convince your partner that overprotectiveness prevents children from building resilience.

For the good of everyone, insist on balancing the expression of your masculine strengths and your partner's feminine strengths. Take the lead to facilitate an authoritative parenting style.

PRACTICE:

Talk to your wife about how she feels when your children are disciplined. Share some of the ideas you read about in this segment of the book.

Ask her, "How can I support you during these challenging moments with the kids?"

Clarify family roles and tasks

Family roles are a contentious issue for many couples these days. This is where your relationship is most at risk from the cultural bug. When the battle for equality penetrates family life, the narrative of fairness runs high and you can become the natural 'unfairness' culprit. In my practice, I frequently hear from men about their combative wives complaining about an unfair division of tasks.

However, once we explore the details of who does more, the picture is not at all black and white. There is much social confusion around gender roles. To address the fairness-victimhood narrative, you must create order in your family roles. You certainly do not want to get bogged down in a discussion about a victimhood narrative or argue with your partner about fairness.

So how do you avoid that?

You clarify your family roles. The more clarity you have in who does what, the fewer conflicts and the less fairness-victimhood narrative you will have.

As men, we are creatures of systems. We are used to a work environment where our jobs, tasks, and positions in the organization are clearly defined. Every worker is accountable to a manager. We need this structure to function at our best.

However, in modern family life, the boundaries of the male role have become blurry, and you may get lost. And when you are not sure what is expected, you may default to avoidance of the throne. If you don't take the leadership role, your partner may end up bossing you around. She resents doing that as much as you do.

The solution is to create order in your respective family roles.

Agree on clearly defined tasks for each of you. She likely has a clearer idea than you about all the necessary household tasks. Perform these tasks with a healthy dose of flexibility and consideration for one another.

For example, take the most explosive moment of each day for many families. After a long and draining day with little kids, wives look forward to their husbands coming home for relief. However, the husbands often look forward to some downtime at home after a long and tiring day at work. This clash of needs often creates tension. Wives bombard their husbands with requests for help and husbands beg for some rest.

When you negotiate with your partner about how to meet both of your needs, a good outcome might be an agreement on who does what during these stressful moments, including how to take turns getting a brief rest. For most men, household tasks don't seem to matter much. Some possible explanations include that these tasks are not paid, performance is not measured, or there is no potential promotion reward like there is in a work environment. But you should be aware that doing these tasks for your partner may matter a lot, and if so, it matters for your relationship.

That's why I encourage you to insist on a clear division of roles and tasks. Your wife may prefer a flexible and intuitive division. When women collaborate in teams, they tend to rely on their sensitivity and responsiveness toward one another, rather than on creating order. But most men operate differently.

Once you establish your tasks, be 100 percent accountable for doing them. This is an opportunity to show how generous and reliable you are. Remember that your wife values the equal sharing of household tasks, so it's important to make your work visible to her. Accountability (as you will soon find) for the fair sharing of tasks is like an insurance policy for your relationship.

PRACTICE:

Consider a household area that you and your wife are both prone to argue about. Negotiate the division of tasks with your wife. Be as specific as possible about what you both want to see happen. Be fully accountable for your task.

Ensure accountability

A couple came to see me, and she said to him: "I have had enough of your swearing." He listened with intent and promised to never swear again. She showed signs of satisfaction and relief. Case closed.

But was it really?!

Of course not. Because swearing was his habit. Habits are hard to break.

So, what do you say to someone who often breaks a commitment on a very important matter for you? This is where the accountability test comes in handy.

I encouraged the woman to ask the man what should happen if he swore again. He reassured her that it wouldn't happen. She accepted his response. But I insisted on her getting an answer "just in case it happens."

He became increasingly agitated because he hoped that the case was closed. He asked with frustration whether he needed to be punished like a kid. I explained that if he chose the consequence and would willingly act on it if he broke his word, then he is not a kid, but a King!

When you agree to be accountable for your actions and take the consequences, this is called accountability. Accountability is an essential expression of a King's energy. Instead of guilt and anger, instead of being blamed or shamed, you maintain your honor by taking ownership of your mistake and paying the consequence you agreed on.

This is how you demonstrate your commitment to your values and your words. By being accountable, you develop the habit of forethought and an ongoing awareness of the consequences of your actions. Accountability will manifest your words, intentions, and plans, just like planting seeds in the soil will make them grow.

When you are accountable, you do something to rectify your mistake. You explain, apologize, compensate, or pay a consequence. While responsibility refers to how you are expected to respond to a task or role, accountability always comes **after** the act and refers to the consequence. So, if you fail to live up to your word, always do something to rectify it.

Partners are often irritated and made angry by each other's repeated bad habits. Saying "sorry" is then not enough to appease the other. Being accountable shows your willingness to break a bad habit due to your care for your partner. You then become more trustworthy and reliable because you demonstrate commitment to your words.

Holding yourself accountable is a powerful expression of your leadership in your family. It shows that your words mean everything to you and you take them seriously. It means that you owe your partner answers and are willing to accept the consequences if you don't act on your words.

Being accountable also implies that you are willing to learn and adapt. It is a mindful attitude towards your actions and their consequences. As a King, things don't just happen to you—you make them happen instead. You are the agent to anything that happens in your environment. Since mistakes are here to teach us (not shame us), your accountability is a fantastic tool for personal growth. Love it!

The accountability test

Let's see how accountability works in practice.

Imagine you agreed with your wife that you would take on the role of making sure the kitchen is left clean before bedtime. After a while, she complains to you about dirt she finds in the morning. You apologize and promise to pay attention to the issue. Fast forward six months, and she is very upset by the many times you have both repeated the complaint-apology-promise-disappointment cycle. Trust is broken.

To rectify this situation, you apply the accountability test. You tell her that if it happens again, you'll pay a consequence you both agree upon.

Selecting the right consequence is an art. You want it to be impactful. Let me give you an example from my own life. Some clients require receipts after their sessions. A few times I forgot to do so. When those clients pursued their receipts, neither of us was happy about it. I told them that if it happened again, I would deduct ten dollars from the cost of the next session. Since I forgot three times, integrating my new habit cost me thirty dollars.

What should the consequence be?

The consequence of a broken commitment in your marriage can be selected either by you or by your wife, preferably by you.

To be both impactful and convincing, choose your consequences with care. Here are a few examples from my clients:

- donate to charity,
- buy her a morning coffee,
- clean the kitchen for one week,
- ban screen time, or
- make a public commitment.

One possible consequence of demonstrating accountability is agreeing to take counseling, privately or together. Women appreciate it when their partners take counseling. Regardless of the outcome, your willingness to own the problem and invest in rectifying it proves your accountability. It also instills hope that things are going to be different.

Each time you prove your accountability, you earn respect as a King.

PRACTICE:

Discuss an issue with your wife that she often complains about. Agree on the change you are willing to make. Once you make a commitment, negotiate the consequence with her if you break it.

Manage financial matters in an orderly manner

Money is second to child rearing as the most contentious issue that couples fight over.

Compared with other areas of family life, men generally are more anxious to see order in how money is spent. In many families (particularly those with mothers who stay at home to raise young children), the man is the primary breadwinner. As such, he feels more in charge of the household finances and more concerned about spending. We can generalize here and say that you tend to be concerned about family finances while your wife is more concerned about your kids' welfare. You both often exaggerate the respective risks.

The answer to your need for security in your family's finances is once again to create order. Individual freedoms need to be balanced with boundaries. Without arrangements and agreement about your family's budget, you both risk running into the red zone of your bank account. If you do, fears will soon build and accusations will fly around the house. In such chaotic situations, men tend to respond with spending restrictions. Too often I hear wives complain about their husbands controlling them by having their hand on the spending 'tap.' Continuously regulating your wife's spending is unreasonable, ineffective, and damaging to your relationship. If your partner feels under your control, she will feel powerless and this will result in anger and resentment. You really don't want that.

Getting your finances in order restores your wife's trust and creates peace of mind. You both need to negotiate and agree on your budget for each important area in your family life. (Search online for sample budgets). You should also agree on regular times to revisit and reassess your budget (2–3 times per year). In this way, your family budgeting process can be similar to one in a successful organization.

If you feel anxious about your finances and your partner feels controlled by you, I recommend agreeing on the structure of your budget first and then letting your wife have full control over the spending. When people are given the power to make free choices within certain limits, they act more responsibly. They are held accountable.

PRACTICE:

Voice your concerns and tell your wife how and why financial order is important for your peace of mind. Stress the point that it's not about controlling, but about gaining a sense of security for all of you as a family.

Negotiate your budget for various spending areas and agree on times to reassess and adjust it.

Create rituals

A famous saying in my Jewish tradition beautifully captures the importance of rituals: "More than the Jewish people have kept the Sabbath (Saturday), the Sabbath has kept the Jewish people." Indeed, weekly rituals that have been performed by Jewish people for thousands of years have strengthened the bonds of families and kept communities alive.

Rituals don't have to be religious or spiritual. What differentiates a ritual from a habit or a routine is its sense of purpose and connectedness. You perform rituals with the intention of connecting to others or something greater than yourself, such as your family, the community, your nation, nature, or God. While anchoring in a certain space and time, you transcend the challenges of your daily routine. Marital rituals create a conscious and intentional relationship because they require your attention and focus, unlike your autopilot. These rituals balance your reactive mode with intentional and meaningful activities of your choice. And when you choose them consciously, these rituals are constructive and positive.

In the midst of your stress and chaos of raising children, romance and intimacy can hardly be spontaneous. You need to be intentional and strategic about them. Otherwise, you both may get caught up in the demanding routines of childrearing and breadwinning. This often results in your relationship being neglected. Your repeated and intentional activities (rituals) guarantee that you cement the marital bond that holds your family together.

Jewish rabbis found a very smart solution to that sore issue centuries ago. They set up rituals around physical connection which give it special meaning and help to guarantee the regularity of sex and intimacy. In an orthodox Jewish community, you will hardly hear a woman complaining about the 'demand' for sex from her husband.

Take the lead and design rituals that take you beyond the mundane tasks and remind you of the big picture of your love and purpose as a family. Here are a few examples of rituals:

- **Kisses on goodbye and reunion**

  These moments of acknowledgment remind you of your strong bond. The goodbye kiss is a statement of "I will miss you" and the reunion kiss is a statement that "I have missed you." Both opportunities should never be missed.

- **Rituals around core values**

  Consider anchoring a certain ritual in your daily or weekly routine that focuses on the importance of a specific value (like friendship, kindness, or gratitude). For example, during dinner, share moments when you felt grateful or experienced kindness.

- **Your special time**

  It's natural for both partners to get carried away by the demands of raising a family. This is a bottom-up impact. As a King, you can create a top-down impact which maintains your commitment to 'our time together.' My friends call their daily catch-up "our mini-dates." Some couples hire a babysitter on a regular basis to guarantee their ritual of 'our special time.'

Commitment to such rituals will prove vital for both keeping your relationship alive and your family intact.

PRACTICE:

Talk to your wife about connection rituals and choose one together. Take the lead in committing to this ritual.

Accept influence

An enlightened leader is one who is open to feedback and influence from the people he leads. This is a core principle in a democratic leadership style. People feel more involved and motivated when they are heard. It is even more critical in the case of a relationship in which men and women are equal in running the family. A partner who is heard and understood is keener on collaborating than resisting. When Gottman was asked to sum up the key messages coming out of his extensive research on couples, he replied that women should turn to their men softly rather than with anger, and men should be willing to accept influence. "Time and again," Gottman and Silver write, "we can separate the happy from the unstable couples based on whether the husband is willing to accept influence from his wife."[55]

If your wife experiences you as defensive, stubborn, controlling, or argumentative, she will feel powerless because her voice matters less. Loss of power breeds resentment. A study of newlywed couples found that wives of disagreeable husbands expressed distress because their husbands were condescending, controlling, inconsiderate, and self-centered. Not surprisingly, spouses of highly disagreeable men tend to be miserable in their marriages, and by the fourth year of marriage many seek separation.[56]

But when you are responsive and reasonably agreeable, she feels empowered—her voice matters. Conflicts go down in intensity and frequency. After all, this is how good friends treat each other. Your flexibility pays off.

During couples therapy, I often see the relief on a wife's face when her man is willing to follow my perspective and advice to respond to her differently. Your partner will similarly feel validated when you respect what she says. Focus not on being right, but on being understanding and accepting. Accepting her input generates the spirits of generosity, consideration, and collaboration. And remember Aristotle's principle of virtue outlined in Chapter Three—find the middle ground between being too pleasing and too controlling. The middle ground creates a sense of equal power, fairness, and mutual consideration.

PRACTICE:

Ask your wife what areas she would like you to be more open to hearing her input. To dare even more, ask her to tell you the area where you could benefit from some personal development. Consider this list of 24 character strengths that are studied in the field of positive psychology:

- creativity
- curiosity
- critical thinking
- gratitude
- hope/optimism
- love of learning
- perspective/wisdom
- bravery
- perseverance
- honesty/integrity
- zest/enthusiasm
- capacity to love/nurture close relationships
- kindness
- social intelligence
- teamwork
- fairness
- leadership
- forgiveness
- modesty/humility
- prudence/caution
- self-regulation/self-discipline
- appreciation of beauty and excellence
- humor/playfulness
- spirituality/purpose

Takeaway messages to activate your King

Your purpose as a King is to create order. With qualities of leadership, sense of agency, clarity, and directedness you are busy creating the future. Children tend to be impulsive and chaotic, and their mothers are affected by that. Your family needs your leadership to consistently and reliably enforce the values and rules you and your wife should agree upon. By creating and maintaining order, you provide your family with the most basic of our psychological needs—security.

Your action plan

- Use the power of your words. Inspire and lead with positive intentions, with Yes.
- Lead your family with vision, values, and rules.
- Prove your commitment to your words through accountability.
- Stick to the agreed rules and roles. It creates trust and security while preventing conflicts.
- Use rituals to enhance meaningful connections with your partner.
- As an enlightened King, be open to accepting your Queen's influence.

5

ACTIVATE YOUR LOVER TO CULTIVATE CONNECTION

*"The lover is related and connected to all things around...
his sensitivity leads him to feel compassionately united with
them. All things are bound to each other in mysterious ways,
inter-connected."*

**— Robert Moore and Douglas Gillette, King, Warrior,
Magician, Lover**

Here is a brief reminder of the Lover identity card that I
described in more detail in Chapter Three.

My identity	I am one with the world and with people. I am connected, I am in my body, I am now. I feel things, I am sensual.
My purpose	To connect with all, to love and share, to enjoy being, and to experience things fully.
How I work	I connect to people. I care. I worship beauty and indulge my senses. I enjoy the moment.

Her voice:

"I am 'feelings,' I deeply feel the experiences of those I love. I feel their joy and their pain.. My sensitivity is both my strength and my weakness. Sometimes I cannot differentiate myself from the people I love. When my boundaries dissolve and I become emotional, I need you to be the strong man who can hold me during my vulnerability. This demonstrates your love and care for me. I want to fully trust that you are there when I need you and that you feel the same way about me. This is how I feel the love between us.

But if you turn away from me or turn against me, it goes straight to my heart and hurts me deeply. I feel misunderstood, alone, and even betrayed. I need to know that I am your first priority, that you are always there for me and that we are connected.

Please stay connected. Always. Communicate with me through any means available. Text messages and phone calls are always welcome. Your hugs are like good drugs.

And please let me know what you need as well! Never shut me out. I feel better when I know all about you because it enables me to support you. Please don't interpret this as controlling, but as caring. I want us to bring out the best in each other so that we can be the family we dream to be."

Lovers speak the language of the heart. The heart reflects being alive, passion, connectedness, and meaning. To communicate the energy of the heart, the Lover will touch, smile, and talk about feelings. He knows how to love, thanks to his capacity to connect. He connects with his own feelings as much as with what others feel. This enables him to relate to others and be sensitive to them. Lovers can touch and move others with their words, humor, creativity, and affection. Their enthusiasm and excitement can be compelling. Nothing can lift the energy of your partner more than your Lover energy.

Connection is the lifeline for your marriage, just like water for your garden. In fact, this connection is your most vital nutrient for both your physical and mental health. Connecting to your wife goes as deep as connecting to yourself, society, and life itself. In his TED Talk and YouTube channel, medical specialist Dr. Dean Ornish preaches the healing power of connection as the medication for many of our ailments.[57] We are injured by relationships, and we are also healed by them. We need connection for thriving just as birds need space for flying.

Like in your garden, you don't wait passively for nature to do its part to flourish. Instead, you build a sturdy irrigation system and cultivate the soil. As a King, you strive to take charge and lead in all areas, including in relationships. Unfortunately, too often I see men leave relationship care to their partners. They wrongly believe that if their partners talk and read so much about relationships, then women must be better at them. They aren't necessarily, just as interest in sports doesn't make you a better football player. Leading in your relationship with your wife doesn't mean that you make either more or less effort. It only means that you keep the idea of cultivating connection in your mind. This means the world to her and makes her feel cared for and loved.

It's highly likely that your wife cultivates her connection with your kids. This is where most of her psychic energy goes, but it is not a deliberate choice! She is merely reacting to the demands of mother nature. As you have probably noticed, children can be emotionally draining. Her attention is often grabbed by matters that are more important right now than her relationship with you.

If one of your kids is suffering, expect a significant impact on her well-being. This impact is one of the most underrated by both couples and professionals. It is often suppressed and goes unnoticed, but an unhappy child goes straight to your partner's sense of worth as a mother. It's painful for her. Your first goal here is to take the perspective of a King, which means not to take it as a sign of neglecting you, but to understand the broader context of her motherly instincts, child development stages, and changing needs. As a King, maintain the system ('order') of your connection.

However, connection doesn't come easy. After all, your male instincts have evolved very differently from her female instincts. "Humans were not designed by natural selection to coexist in mating bliss," Buss wrote in *Evolution of Desire*. "They were designed for individual survival and genetic reproduction."[58] Any attempt to blur the gender differences is ridiculous from both the evolutionary and biological perspectives. These differences make both of you virtually an unnatural match because there are too many areas with potential for clashes.

Intimacy between a man and a woman is pretty much a development of the last hundred years. For our ancient instincts, this change is like a brand-new upgrade. We are all still adjusting. She now mostly relies on one person only and he is a man. You are now required to replace her whole community of female supporters. Both of your instincts cry for 'help.'

This modern intimacy is the new evolutionary project for men. Male tasks in the old days involved risking their bodies more, but for a man in the 21st century, risking the heart is the new frontier. The new Warrior is the 'connected Warrior,' whose main challenges are to meet his partner at the heart level and express his needs and vulnerabilities authentically. For the old Warrior, this vulnerability was a taboo, but for the modern Warrior sharing vulnerability with his wife can be his strength. It is an important strength that many modern women are seeking in a partner.

Your reason to adapt is not succumbing to pressure from society but rather serving your own values as a King! These are the Lover-related values such as care, support, loyalty, and trust. This is the King's top-down approach: values overrule instincts and emotions. Each time you cultivate connection with your partner, you cement your marriage. What could be more important than that?

Connection builds your marriage while disconnection may harm its healthy functioning and long-term sustainability. Partners caught up by their strong emotional reactions during conflicts fail to see that what truly matters is not what just happened, but what did not happen in the last few weeks or months. Loss of connection (affection, time together, sharing) is the virus behind relationship 'inflammation'—fights, anger, fear, resentment.

But when partners feel connected, everyone in the family feels more secure. This leads to more peace, joy, and openness. Everyone is more accepting, forgiving, and tolerant towards one another. Conflicts are not as threatening, and they are resolved much faster.

When you cultivate connection, you invest in the emotional bank account of your family. Any pleasant interaction (such as affection or an act of kindness) is a deposit, while any unpleasant interaction (such as blaming or fighting) is a withdrawal. To make relationships flourish, there is a healthy ratio of 5:1 between pleasant and unpleasant interactions. Gottman describes this formula as his most important research finding.[59] One unpleasant interaction is so powerful that you need five pleasant ones to balance it out. This ratio explains why it is essential for you to be conscious and intentional in your marriage. Unpleasant interactions occur anyway, but the pleasant ones require a proactive approach to cultivate them; this is where your leadership is needed.

But before we go after positivity, let's understand why and how negativity is so powerful. Understanding the origins of fear and anger in your relationship makes it easier for you to handle them. You will soon realize that those feelings are not as personal as you both perceive them to be. Instead, your brains follow a universal and deeply ingrained script—welcome to your attachment brain.

Brain for love

Your attachment brain is the engine behind any drama you experience in your intimate relationship. The very unromantic truth about this brain is that it is driven by fears and it makes us constantly on the lookout for emotional security. This security is achieved through connection.

This attachment brain explains how we have survived as the human species. We are born entirely dependent. Our first task in life is to build trust because we are so vulnerable. At around 9–10 months, we realized that we were separate and alone in this world, and we began to develop separation anxiety. Each time we were left alone, we fought to restore connection with our caregivers. Our attempts took the form of crying, screaming, tantrums, and rage. Only years later when we fall in love do we realize that we have never outgrown this desire to stay close to an attachment person. Embarrassingly, even some of our old strategies to protest and restore connection to our attachment person are still around. This explains why love can hurt so much, and why at times it brings out the worst in people.

We are wired to seek connection in order to feel loved and secure. The intensity of the attachment which we felt towards our caregivers when we were toddlers can reappear in our romantic relationships. Emotionally, we 'use' our partners in a similar way to how we 'used' our parents: we maintain emotional and physical closeness, we reach out at times of distress, we miss each other when we are apart, and we count on our partners to be there for us when we explore the world. Our partners become our safe haven, the place to go when we need support, and that one person who knows all about us. We trust our partners to be there for us in times of need. This is the person about whom we wonder "ARE you there for me?" According to renowned researcher and relationship educator, Sue Johnson, ARE is an acronym for accessible, responsive, engaged.[60]

When our partners meet our needs, we feel secure and calm. But when connection is lost, we experience anxiety, powerlessness, and isolation. The impact is profound on our sense of self, and on our mood, clarity, and productivity. Our distress then spills over to other areas of life—parenting, work, hobbies, and friends.

No wonder conflicts provoke anxiety when there is so much at stake. Disagreements are unavoidable, but the ways that each partner manages them can make or break the relationship. The most common conflict pattern is 'demand-withdraw.' One partner (often the wife) demands, protests, complains, and criticizes, while the other (often the husband) withdraws, avoids, and stonewalls. This gender difference is a highly consistent finding in research.[61]

When managing conflicts, it seems like men have swapped one dysfunctional strategy—controlling—with another (withdrawing). Modern family rules require men to settle differences through talking and negotiation. Many men find themselves at a loss without any skills to work through their feelings and uncomfortable confrontations. They tend to disengage and avoid instead. Tragically, the more that men disengage, the more their partners feel disconnected and lonely. In their desperation, women tend to act in ways that further push their men away, such as criticizing, complaining, demanding, and attacking.

Partners in relationship distress are often locked in this rigid and vicious cycle. The more he does his dysfunctional part, the more she does her dysfunctional part. If not addressed in time, this ever-widening spiral may destroy the relationship.

The demand-withdraw cycle reflects two primal emotions—female anxiety and male shame. In clumsy attempts to restore secure attachment, both genders achieve the exact opposite outcome. Men disconnect from their partners only to see them become even more anxious. Women criticize and blame their partners only to make them feel ashamed, and further avoid and hide. Since men tend to default to withdrawal during conflicts, and since this response hurts women so badly, it is essential for *The Good Husband* model to circuit-break the vicious cycle.

How?

Always, always, always try to remain engaged.

This should be your relationship mantra.

Always keep in mind that avoidance and the 'silent treatment' throw your partner into states of helplessness and despair. This 'solution' to feeling hurt will create a mega problem for you—it will destroy her trust in you and ultimately your marriage.

Yes, when you are hurt, you are angry and it can be tough. Yet, this is where you can demonstrate your masculine power as the Lover by staying connected, being present, and remaining committed. Don't 'check out' when someone you love hurts you. To love is to stay close despite any hardships. Your wife needs to know that you are there for her. (To handle aggression, you will consult your Warrior. See Chapter Seven.)

When we are dependent on another person, we are vulnerable. Our strategy to overcome vulnerability is trust. However, it can take very little to break trust. This is the case for your wife when she relies on you. Loving is trusting you. She trusts you to be there for her when she needs you. Each time you disconnect with her, and each time you are not available when she needs you, it is a micro betrayal for her. It hurts her deeply.

Don't delude yourself that you are there for her just because you are physically home. She can sense in your body language if you are not with her. She craves your presence in the form of emotional responsiveness, in how attuned you are to her, and in how you see her. When she talks, be sensitive to any expression of her feelings. Note her body language or words and respond with emotional attunement. This is something she likely does very well with your kids. The following statements—expressed in a soft tone—are examples of demonstrating emotional attunement to her feelings:

- "What's happening?"
- "You look exhausted."
- "I see you are sad."
- "Let me hug you."
- "How can I help?"
- "Why are you upset?"
- "Sounds like you worry about it."
- "What do you need?"

When she is upset, she needs your full attention. Her intense feeling is a call for your support and attunement. Emotional attunement is the art of the feminine. As you learn to attune, you integrate feminine power within you and become a far more balanced man. Don't stress if you don't fully live up to her emotional attunement standards. It can suffice to be aware of how important your emotional attunement is for her, and to respond from time to time with the above statements.

Enemies of connection

When your Lover energy gets out of balance, you are at risk of falling into addictive and obsessive habits such as alcohol and drug use, watching porn, or gambling. These habits are extremely disturbing for your wife and sadly are common complaints. For her, these habits make her feel as if you have another relationship that sucks your attention and energy, alters your mood, and reduces you to being like a little kid that is a victim of his uncontrolled impulses.

As you can imagine, these habits only add to her anxiety and stress. If you have any of these bad habits, they will make you unpredictable and unreliable. In extreme cases, your wife will feel like she needs to deal with another child instead of receiving support from you. She is likely to protest at the start, then look at you helplessly, then lose respect for you and finally, you will lose her love. When that happens, you will soon discover that the emotional pain you temporarily escaped with your habits is nothing compared to the pain of losing your connection with your wife. You will lose your center, your focus, your marriage, and your money.

If you have any addictive and obsessive habits, deal with your demons urgently. You will find some tips on how to do that in the next chapter in which we discuss the power of your Magician.

THE LOVER IN ACTION

These are the tools you will need to activate your inner Lover:

- connect by doing,
- talk your way to her heart,
- communicate authentically,
- adopt the soft-start tool,
- use the magic of touching,
- get unstuck with sex, and
- nourish 'being.'

Let's look at each tool in more detail.

Connect by doing

Connecting via talking and touching often comes with some hurdles. Sharing by doing activities and hobbies instead is the easiest and safest way to restore and strengthen your connection with each other. Doing activities together can revitalize your connection for several reasons:

1. They take you back to earlier days when you built your friendship through having fun times together.
2. They involve positive feelings such as joy, interest, and laughter.
3. They engage the creative, playful, and free-spirited child within you both, taking your mind away from serious tasks.
4. They build memories for you both to reflect on and share with friends.
5. They may add meaning and a sense of belonging for you both if done in the context of a group or community.

Sharing activities such as hiking, dancing, or enjoying the arts (e.g., the theater or live music) is almost guaranteed to be successful in revitalizing your connection. Research on the impact of such pleasant moments shows how their longer-term impact far exceeds their short-lived good feelings. They build resilience and open the mind for learning.[62] They boost your relationship and well-being. So, take the lead in finding the time to do activities together that you both enjoy.

PRACTICE:

Here are some ideas for activities. Discuss them with your partner. Consider trying out two new activities and plan the time for them. Take the initiative—don't wait for her.

- Going to a movie.
- Going to live sports or entertainment.
- Going out with friends.
- Dining out.
- Traveling/Planning a vacation.
- Driving to the country.
- Hiking
- Playing (e.g., cards, a puzzle, Scrabble, bowling, pool, darts, sport games).
- Cycling.
- Massaging each other gently (foot, neck, back).
- Going for a walk locally.
- Doing a hobby together.
- Nature activities (e.g., rock climbing, scuba diving, snorkeling, skiing).
- Taking dance lessons.
- Taking a personal development course or learning together.

Talk your way to her heart

Gender differences in conversation style are well documented. They are the source of many frictions and... comedies. In her book *You Just Don't Understand*, sociologist Deborah Tannen describes this as a mismatch between your "report-talk" and her "rapport-talk."[63] You talk to convey knowledge, solutions, and opinions which confirm your status. You listen functionally with goals in mind or the desire to fix problems. You may say impatiently, "just tell me what you want me to do" or "so what is your point?"

Well, her point is connection! According to Tannen, this is the main motivation behind female talking. Women's main interest tends to be in people, relationships, and feelings. Their primal desire to connect is fueled by their primal need for security. A communication mismatch occurs when your wife engages her heart in conversation while you engage your brain. The wise thing to do is to 'sync' with her communication style.

Tannen suggests looking at these different styles as cultural differences, and then adopting a tolerant multicultural perspective: Neither of you is wrong or crazy; your natural communication styles just tend to be different. As a man, you are likely to be used to a world of hierarchy and status in which you are rewarded for your skills and knowledge. But when you come back home, you may be surprised to find a lack of consideration for your professional skills. Your wife and children will expect a different communication style—one that is not driven by your status or smart brain. They demand your heart! They long for your Lover to show up, presenting qualities such as these:

- connection before information,
- affection before advice,
- feeling before fixing, and
- being before doing.

Men who hopelessly use their brain to communicate when their heart is needed will be ineffective. As the saying goes: "If all you have is a hammer, you only see nails."

In ancient times, when men used their physical strength for hunting and fighting, women used language to communicate with their community of women and children. This is where women honed their verbal and interpersonal skills. It was a matter of survival. Talking helps women to stay connected with their children and communities, and it helps them to feel secure.

Talking to you will help your wife feel secure with you. She wants to know all about you to ensure that you are investing your resources in your marriage. Knowledge is power, and secrets are threats. And she also wants you to know about her. Knowing each other is how you both show you care.

Research completely backs her up. Studies of couples in long and happy marriages have discovered that they tend to engage in a unique daily ritual. They spend about twenty minutes catching up with each other about their main events and experiences each day. This ritual enables them to know everything about each other. To know is to care. Knowing is loving.[64]

Yet, there is much more for you in talking your way into your partner's heart than just knowing her. Connecting emotionally through talking is like foreplay for women. It goes to their hearts, strengthens trust and opens them to physical connection and sex. Your wife wants to release emotionally just as you want to release sexually. As you respond to her need for emotional connection, you are more likely to get her to respond to your sexual needs. She is all for mutual consideration. It is 'fair.'

PRACTICE:

Discuss the 'catch-up ritual' with your wife. Suggest allocating 20 minutes each day to talk about what happened to you both during the day.

One of the biggest pitfalls in such a conversation is that a woman often worries that her man is not listening to her, while he worries that she won't stop talking.

If this is the case for you, I suggest you structure the conversation. Use a timer and agree on how you run the conversation. When your need for order is matched with her need for connecting, you will reach a win-win solution.

Communicate authentically

Men are often confronted when asked to discuss their feelings. They tend to struggle with both recognizing their body sensations and naming them. Their emotional literacy is generally not as developed as their partner's, but they are increasingly being pressured to share their vulnerability in contemporary society. Sadly, this pressure often turns into bullying and shaming, even at the hands of other men who have recently been 'enlightened.'

This confrontational approach often results in the opposite outcome— men feel exposed and shamed, and close themselves further. I have witnessed this many times in counseling sessions and men's groups. I see traces of the cultural bug here: drop your 'ideology' and start sharing your vulnerability with us. When I see a man on TV being asked "how are you feeling?" I cringe for him. A woman surely values when her man is successful and provides well. But the very traits that enable him to do so are not as compatible with emotional intimacy. When she seeks emotional closeness, she may complain that her man is not sharing his feelings with her. The man may feel confused and helpless.

Many people fail to understand the challenge of communicating your feelings, including the largest body of psychologists (as we learned in Chapter One). When you try to learn authentic communication skill, it is essential to start with self-understanding and self-acceptance.. This is not easy for most men.

However, this skill will enable you to express what you feel and need in a way that is better aligned with your values. Men don't enjoy being angry, aggressive, or avoidant. They do so only because they generally lack the skill to express their vulnerability effectively. The paradox is that expressing vulnerability virtually gives you power. Why? Firstly, you are not being reactive when you are vulnerable, but on top of things instead—your King is in charge. Secondly, people are likelier to listen and respond to what you want when you express your vulnerability. Your other options (getting angry or withdrawing) are losing strategies. They expose you as weak, not strong. This weakness happens to you when you fail to convey effectively and authentically what you feel and need.

Our vulnerability is not a weakness, but an existential condition as human beings. We all have fear. Evolution has made sure you are equipped with the right instincts for your tasks as a male protector and provider: act, don't feel; hold yourself together, and suppress your vulnerability. This explains why it may take you longer to turn inside and discover your feelings.

It is what it is. No apology, no shame! As a soldier and consultant in the Israeli army in my earlier years, I could see how our best soldiers were the ones who talked the least about their feelings. I salute, rather than condemn them.

However, from time to time it's only natural to feel needy, helpless, and powerless. But the way we cope with our vulnerabilities will make us weak or strong. In the context of your marriage, coping means making sure your partner knows and considers your needs. You can't control what she does with your message, but you can make sure that she gets it.

To speak about your vulnerability is to speak the language of the heart—the language of the Lover. There are three key statements in speaking vulnerability:

1. "I feel,"
2. "I need," and
3. "I ask."

For example: "I feel annoyed when you leave the desk messy. I need your consideration here. (I ask you to) please keep it tidy for me."

Another one: "I feel hurt when you speak to me in that tone. I need respect not criticism. Please use softer language."

Adopting the Soft-Start tool

To make it easier for my clients to learn this authentic communication language, I share the following soft-start tool. It is designed to change the course of conflict from a harsh start to a soft one because the opening tone dictates how the interaction unfolds. Your interaction is like a train: It follows the track you put it on. The starting point is crucial to where it ends up. When upset, one partner may turn harshly toward the other so that matters quickly escalate. This tool will help you both to structure your interaction so that you start gently.

The Soft-Start Tool

"When I saw or heard..."
(share an observation/fact, not an interpretation).

"I reacted by..."
(becoming angry / withdrawing / attacking / being shocked / laughing).

"But deep inside I felt..."
(sad / hurt / lonely / worried / scared / ashamed / disappointed / betrayed).

"Because I started to imagine or think..."
(your beliefs, assumptions).

"Yet, what I truly need and long for is to feel..."
(secure / connected / supported / respected / appreciated / understood / accepted).

"To help me, please..."
(Be specific about what your partner can do rather than stop doing.)

And here is a short version.

The Soft-Start Tool (short)

When... (X happened), I felt...
(sad / hurt / lonely / worried / scared / ashamed / disappointed / betrayed).

I need to feel...
(secure / / connected / supported / respected / appreciated / understood / accepted / considered).

Can you please...
(Be specific and positive.)

PRACTICE:

Keep an image of this soft-start tool on your phone and share it with your partner. It is best to practice it in simple situations first. Ask her to do this exercise with you a few times. Remember that the tool is not aimed at resolving a problem, only to set up the opening accord of the conversation. If one of you senses some tension around an issue, you may suggest "can I use the soft-start tool to talk about it?"

Use the magic of touching

It was through touch that we first experienced life, connection, and communication, and it was through touch that we developed trust. As babies, we needed touch in order to thrive, and it remains highly impactful throughout our lives. Physical connection defines the identity and boundaries of any couple. It is the hallmark of your closeness with your partner. To the public, it is a statement about your bond. We only allow physical connection access to the person we trust the most because our body harbors our innermost, intimate, and vulnerable parts.

The need for touch is met uniquely by a spouse. When such a primal need is expected to be met by a partner, it gives them a great deal of power. It makes sense why partners in a touch-starved marriage are so sad, worried, and powerless. Lack of physical connection can be devastating to marriage. As the Lover, you really want to get this connection right.

Touch is the natural language of the Lover. By touching her, you respond to her basic need to feel desired. If she is desired by you, then it means you are invested in her, and this goes straight to the heart of the matter. It is the leading principle in everything you do as a *Good Husband*—making your wife feel secure and wanted.

As the feminine side of the mating game, your partner will likely take the more passive and receptive role. She is waiting for you to initiate and lead in your physical connection. She wants to feel desired, but unfortunately, a woman rarely explains to her man how he can make her feel that way. Perhaps she feels that explaining this spoils the occasion or puts her in a vulnerable position. Her dream is that you spontaneously do what you did during your dating days. You need to figure that out for yourself. Here are some hints.

Touch will change the chemistry of her brain, as Brizendine explains in her book *The Female Brain*.[65] Touch makes her release oxytocin, that magic hormone linked to basic activities that connect human beings—breast-feeding, attachment, empathy, trust, sex, and prosocial behaviors. One important effect of oxytocin is calming down the amygdala, that part of your brain responsible for the 'fight or flight' response. Each time you touch your wife, you can help her to feel calmer, safer, and closer to you.

As body language, touch has its nuances, and it requires sensitivity. Consider the three levels of touch to be like gears in a car. Start with level one, or affectionate touch, then move to sensual touch, and finally to erotic touch. Most women like lots of affection with the occasional sensual touch such as a stroke to the buttocks, a kiss on the neck, and so on. When your woman receives random acts of affectionate touch from you throughout the day, she is more receptive to being touched on the erogenous zones of her body. This progression makes her feel more like your heart object rather than a sex object. You will see and feel her as a whole person, and she will appreciate you for it. Sex for her is more about your relationship. In that sense, you may regard most practices in this book as your foreplay!

Touch is so impactful, effortless, and enjoyable that you can easily regard it as your best return on investment. In fact, I have developed the touch 'formula' for best returns. It's a kind of playful but beneficial strategy. I call it the "180/10 formula." You can follow it by devoting a total of at least 180 seconds a day to touching your wife, and spreading those touches over 10 different interactions. Even if sex is not the end result, you will both enjoy the impact. It serves you both as a means to an end (sex) and as an end in itself (the expression of connection). The impact is always positive.

PRACTICE:

Ask your wife to show you five ways she would like to be touched by you during the day. When she demonstrates each way to you, feel the impact and register the way she touches you. Then go ahead and playfully show her every day how committed you are to showing her affection. Consider the "180/10 formula" as a guide.

Get unstuck with sex

I approach this topic with some dread. I am aware there are so many men who are sexually starved in their marriage and desperate for some 'strategies.' This might be the main topic of interest for them. Yet, we must keep in mind that nothing we say here can cover the variety of issues that couples struggle with. Restoring regular sex with your partner after a long break may take some effort and patience.

What makes women sexually responsive is one of the biggest mysteries. The theory is that if you only treat her well and help around the house, she will be more responsive. It sounds good for blogs and TV programs, but it doesn't always work like that. For example, there are women who engage in hot sex shortly after discovering their men are having an affair or even after being assaulted by them.

However, it is clear that your wife holds the key to how satisfying your sex life is. If she needs to initiate or seek sex with you, then your relationship is in real danger because she doesn't have the same resilience and tolerance for rejection that you do. Rejecting her can have a devastating impact. This is another example of a 'double standard' created by mother nature. The game is that she is the object of your desire and you are constantly challenged to get her to say 'yes.'] This is her natural power, so give her reasons to use it.

"Mission accomplished"

A young couple in their late twenties came to see me because they had only had sex four times over the last year. She was depressed, and he was very caring and understanding.

I invited him to share what it was like for him not to have sex for such a long time.

"I miss you," he said.

"Oh, I feel awful... " she replied with tears of guilt and sadness.

"It's okay darling, I'm fine," he answered in a soft and caring tone.

At that stage, I intervened: "No, you are not fine!" I explained how the lack of sex may harm their relationship.

By the end of the session, I encouraged the young man to be more goal-oriented and get to sex as soon as possible. I asked him to text me "mission accomplished" when it was done and they both laughed.

A moment later, she stunned us both by saying: "For some strange reason it turned me on when you said 'mission accomplished'." Another example of the complex and confusing nature of the females' sex life. Two weeks later, the man texted me "Mission accomplished."

This story demonstrates the tragic misunderstanding among many modern men. They play the feminine 'tune' of being kind and caring, only to realize their partners ultimately need more of their masculine energy. "Desire me with passion," they say.

Sex is a very complex matter. It is susceptible to personal history, biological forces, and cultural influences. Tragically, many relationships unravel because they don't deal with these challenges successfully. They fail to use the immense potency of sexual connection to cement their bond. This is the same potency that launched them into the space of love and helped them create a family.

At this stage, you may ask, "Why don't you say that to my wife?" Indeed, men tend to feel far more sexually frustrated than women. But any avoidance from your wife in this area should not discourage you. There is much you can do to improve your sex life in your capacity as the Lover. I personally didn't do a good job in this realm as a young husband. I felt stuck and helpless. It took me years to realize how different it could have been. You can now benefit from some important lessons I have learned.

Lesson 1: Keep the topic alive

A mismatch of desire between partners (particularly while raising young kids) is natural and very common. What is less natural is the attitude of denial by both husbands and wives. Women may assertively say "I don't feel like it" with the expectation that it is okay to say no, and that their men should sort themselves out... Men tend to helplessly resign themselves to this message while resorting to their instant online porn solution.

Yet, sharing a bed without having sex over a long time leaves its impact. You both sense the impact but prefer to deny and suppress it instead of addressing it. As despair sinks in, your bond slowly unravels. Before too long, you begin to fight over all kinds of petty things, and you don't even understand why you are so reactive towards each other. It would never occur to you to neglect your children in such a way, but let me tell you the truth: you do harm them if you both neglect your sex life. How? Just consider the short- and long-term effects.

Recall your emotional bank account—sex is the mega-dollar that you deposit in it. You both need to wake up to this reality. A poor sex life empties emotional bank accounts because partners feel disconnected, rejected, guilty, worried, and ultimately insecure. Denying it means letting the relationship die. For you as a man, sexual connection means a great deal. Sex makes you come alive, so keep this topic alive!

In his book *Evolution of Desire,* the evolutionary psychologist David Buss says: "depriving a man of sex may eliminate the reproductive dividends on the investment that he has extended in obtaining his wife."[66] These "dividends" go deep into your soul to make you feel accepted, valued, fulfilled, and connected to life itself. To help your wife understand the impact of sex 'starving' on you, ask her to imagine one week without sharing her emotions. Your sexual offloading is the equivalent of her emotional offloading. Both are essential for your respective well-being. These are the gifts you owe each other—to contain and hold the other for your respective primal needs.

In the days after having sex with your wife, you may feel more connected, energized, and enthusiastic about how you respond to her requests. These facts often go unnoticed because attention tends to be more easily affected by what's wrong in a relationship. It's a good idea to draw your wife's attention to what makes your relationship happier. She may be carried away by her reactivity—her feelings and moods—while ignoring the very positive impact of being intimate.

Sex is not just about 'because I feel,' but also about 'what purpose it's for, and what goals it serves.' Unfortunately, many modern young women don't receive wisdom from their elders. Instead, social media messages that ridicule men's 'obsession' with sex distort their perception and validate their unwillingness to respond to 'demands' for sex. "You are a liberated woman so feel free to say no!" As a man, dare to confront the folly in this 'cultural bug' attitude. Her true power is in what she says 'yes' to, rather than in being in opposition. As a Queen, she can lead rather than react to your 'demands' for sex; she can see that being intimate with you is a way to express her values, such as caring about your relationship and your family.

Your desire for sex should be acknowledged and celebrated, not dismissed or ridiculed. The testosterone in your body represents the gift and wisdom of Mother Nature. Listen to it, don't suppress it. When you keep this topic alive, you do so on behalf of your **family**.

Use the King to approach sex from the upper, not lower, part of your body. That is, from the desire to connect, rather than to satisfy your penis. Make it about you and your partner, not just you. When I ask couples what they value the most about sex, the most common answers are: "to get close and feel connected and emotionally nourished," and "to show my love and make my partner feel special."

PRACTICE:

Start a conversation with your wife. Consider reading this segment of the book to her and share your thoughts with each other.

Lesson 2: Speak the heart

Broaching the sex topic can be intimidating. However, as explained earlier in this chapter, the best way to handle vulnerability is to communicate authentically by using the language of the heart. Here are a sample of authentic expressions of your desire:

- "I miss being with you."
- "I would like to connect tonight."
- "Let's go and have a cuddle."

- "I want to feel your body against mine."
- "Can I make you feel good tonight?"
- "I would love to touch your sexy body."
- "I am longing to be with you."
- "Can we get together tonight?"

After any continuous refusal, you may say:

- "It's quite sad for me that we don't connect more often."
- "We haven't been intimate for a while. It worries me."
- "I am worried about our relationship."
- "I am unhappy with how we lack intimacy."
- "I am afraid you are losing me with your continuous rejection."

Have you noticed what word I didn't use? Sex! This is because 'sex' may come across as **your** agenda, rather than **our** agenda. Choose language that will attune to your wife's needs. Some women are aroused by explicit language. So, think and speak to enhance your connection.

Here is how one of my clients expressed his needs to his partner. He used the "soft-start" tool explained earlier in this chapter.

- "When we are not intimate for a long time,
- "On the surface I withdraw and become quiet.
- "But deep inside I feel helpless and hurt by your constant rejection. I am really worried about our relationship.
- "My mind then starts to think that maybe you have given up on us and you no longer care.
- "What I truly long for is to connect with you, and for you to understand how this issue matters to me and how I feel

so bad when we don't connect sexually. I long for the joy of being with you.

- "You could help by showing more care, and by taking the sexual initiative or responding to my initiative. Please give priority to our sex life."

PRACTICE:

Consider these statements as your guide the next time you want to discuss sex with your wife. Share with her authentically how you feel.

Lesson 3: 'De-shame' sexuality

Our sex lives are the most sensitive, private, and secretive aspect of our relationships. It is natural for most human beings to carry a good dose of vulnerability, inhibition, and shame in this area. No wonder partners don't find it easy to talk about this topic, not even with their therapists. As a therapist myself, it took me years to approach this topic comfortably with couples. The healing of this shame is to recognize it, normalize it, and accept it with empathy.

The shame around sexuality is primal. The myth of the Garden of Eden tells the story of how shame was born when Adam and Eve were expelled. The famous image of fig leaves covering and hiding their private parts symbolizes shame. Together with the amazing gift of self-awareness, we have also received the virus of shame. Once you bring light into the dark basement of shame, you are more aware of how shame works and more open to exploring sexual issues. Each time you expose yourself to the topic by reading, talking, and educating yourself about sex, you de-shame it. You walk another stair down the basement towards sexuality where those scary gremlins lie happily next to some wonderful treasures. Enjoy the treasures while smiling at the gremlins!

> ## PRACTICE:
>
> Use educational tools such as videos and books to inspire a healthy attitude towards sexuality. For example, keep a book next to your bed that illustrates different sex positions. Occasionally read a few lines and talk about some of the sexual positions in the book with your partner.

Lesson 4: Fan the flames of desire

Throughout this book, we stress how important it is to respond to your wife's need for security. Yet, even when you do an excellent job as a *Good Husband* (such as being reliable, connected, and supportive), she may still not be keen on sex.

Why is that?

In her book *Mating in Captivity*, Esther Perel offers an interesting answer: The conditions of 'captivity' contradict desire because repetition numbs. Love and attachment require routine, commitment, and security, but for desire to be sparked, your woman needs contradicting conditions that create healthy tension. For example, novelty, diversity, surprise, risk, distance, mystery, the unexpected, or being 'naughty' and 'selfish.' Perel says "It's remarkable to me how a sudden threat to the status quo, such as an affair or even a good fight, can suddenly ignite desire. There's nothing like the fear of loss to make those old shoes look new again."[67]

The opposite to that "fear of loss" is not more security but taking you for granted. If she takes you for granted, it's because there is no healthy tension. You have somehow made her believe that you are okay without sex. To ignite healthy tension, discuss the ramifications for your relationship if she is not sexually engaged with you. To fan the flames of desire, you both need healthy emotional tension. Healthy tension acts like air for your sexual fire.

PRACTICE:

Turn your sex life into something adventurous, playful, and surprising. Spice up your atmosphere or environment with novelty and changes. For best results, consider an overnight stay at a hotel or in nature. With young kids around, home can be like the working space in a factory. Time away is the best enabler for replenishing your sex life.

Lesson 5: Letters can make magic

Sometimes the filters of listening are so contaminated that partners only hear their interpretation and perception of what you say, rather than what is actually said. Written messages are a powerful tool to bypass this barrier. One partner takes the time to design the message, while the other takes time to digest it. Further, written messages are documents that can be kept or shared with others. They force different perspectives and objectivity while they are being read.

I often use this tool with my clients to convey messages to family members. Here is a letter I helped Paul write to his wife Jane (pseudonyms). They had been married 8 years and their kids were 5 and 2. The last time they had had sex was 6 months ago.

Dear Jane,

I'm writing this letter to you to share my feelings about our sex life. I know that this is hard for us to discuss, so I hope with writing we can clarify what we really feel and need without any blame and defensiveness. I don't want you to feel bad, only to understand where I am coming from.

It has been a while since last time you showed an interest in sex and this is very concerning for me. I miss being with you. I feel rejected, sad, and disconnected. You don't make any suggestion that I could work with, so I am helpless and not sure what to do.

It worries me that if we stay like that for too long, it may damage the trust between us. I am worried about our future.

I know that there are many issues at the moment that keep your mind and body away from sex. I understand that. But it also means away from me, away from yourself, away from our relationship. The impact is really big on all of us. Let's not deny. I feel like I am only partially alive. Not connected to the woman I love. It is upsetting for me to write this to you.

I know that it may take more than a few steps to make you ready and I am happy to help. But I need to know that you care. Please don't give up on us. If you care about us please talk to me about the topic or make suggestions to improve. I hope we can restore our connection and enjoy each other.

Love you always.

Paul

It shouldn't surprise you that Jane was moved by the letter. A powerful and heartfelt conversation ensued. Shortly after, they resumed sex.

PRACTICE:

If you feel stuck in your sex life, take inspiration from the content of the above letter and design your own message to your wife. Not exactly a writer? Consider sending her an image of this letter with your comments attached to it.

Nourish 'being'

Your masculine energy is naturally expressed through 'doing'— working, fixing, building, acting, protecting, achieving, competing, and more. Unfortunately, men who are very successful 'doers' often find themselves out of balance with 'being.' That is, they neglect aspects of life such as connecting to their family and friends, spending time on leisure, the arts, nature, and more. Such neglect often results in poor mental and physical health.

As a successful and productive man, you may regard the time you invest in your own well-being as less important. After all, it doesn't bring you any 'measurable results.' This is a very common mistake men make. They perceive the currency of life to be money and material gains rather than experiences such as joy, peace, and meaningful life. They look down on concepts such as happiness. They often leave it to their wives. "I just want you to be happy," they may say to their partners.

'Being' is about the joy we can find in the present moment. Our 'being' activities are not aimed at any future results or benefits, but at making us feel good now. If the desire for 'having' is satisfied by more things, the desire for 'being' is satisfied through connection to your most important assets—your family and friends. Research on happiness shows that money is only important when matters of survival are at stake.[68] For most of us in the West, the critical factor linked to our well-being is the quality and quantity of our relationships. Your wife acts on this factor when she cultivates a network of friends around your family.

You have two excellent reasons to invest in your 'being.' Firstly, your 'being' is the engine that drives everything you do. When your 'being' is well, you are healthy, vital, focused, curious to learn, and... more productive!

Secondly, feeling happy is your very basic right. You fulfill it now, not in the future. In her book *The Top Five Regrets of the Dying*, Bronnie Ware shares what people told her while nearing the end of their life: They wished they had worked less and stayed more in touch with family and friends instead. They wished they had let themselves be happier.[69]

An interesting take on the difference between these two aspects of 'doing' and 'being' can be found in the book *The Ancestral Mind by* Harvard Medical school researcher Gregg Jacobs.[70] Jacobs describes two minds: thinking and ancestral. The thinking mind is analytical, abstract, detached from experience, socially conditioned, set apart from others and nature, and eager to control. The ancestral mind is non-verbal, emotionally connected, experiential, holistic and integrated, and here now.

Our ancestral mind holds the key to our well-being. To activate it, we need to engage in activities that take us away from our busy minds and back to the present moment. For example:

- connecting to our children and community,
- listening to or playing music,
- walking in nature,
- getting playful and laughing, and
- meditating.

Special attention should be paid to your body. While your mind can take you to the past and future, your body is always in the here and now. Connecting to your body is anchoring your life. Your body holds the wisdom of evolution. To treat it kindly is to do the wise thing. But men are notoriously neglectful towards their bodies. They fail to understand that "the body is the shadow of the soul." Body and mind are interconnected.

A sense of vitality and health in your body is reflected in your mood and productivity. Both metaphorically and literally, your body is your baby, and should be treated as such. It deserves your utmost care. Neglect of your body is a betrayal by your inner Lover. In your capacity as a Lover, develop the habit of treating your body with love.

PRACTICE:

Set a routine for yourself which helps you connect to 'being.' Replenish friendships and reach out to people around you. Ask yourself each day "How did I take care of my body and my being today?"

Troubleshoot

"Her tears upset me."

When your woman is in distress or crying, it may evoke a strong reaction in you. Some men may feel so helpless and worried that they end up reacting to their own distress instead of tuning in to their partner's hurt. In their frustration, these men either try to fix the problem unsuccessfully and get angrier, or they withdraw. This response only makes matters worse.

Your partner's distress provides you with the chance to put the golden rule of 'always stay engaged' into practice. Slow down in such moments, restrain yourself, and focus on her. Staying present, even without words, means a lot to her. Connect before fixing, be present before doing.

"I am not comfortable with face-to-face emotional intimacy."

Emotionally intimate conversations often confront men. Some men would rather suppress than raise an emotional issue. While women tend to prefer face-to-face emotional intimacy, men tend to prefer side-by-side. If you relate to that, consider what works for you rather than withdraw altogether from an intimate conversation. For example, you may initiate the talk while walking, driving, or lying down in bed.

"It is an easy fix with porn"

Internet porn is a modern pandemic to the male psyche. The instant dose of dopamine that lifts the mood for a few minutes is irresistible to many men. No wonder it creates addiction with severe ramifications on relationships, and physical and mental health. The secrecy, shame, and concealment block any open conversation. A wife's denial only helps with the concealment.

If your porn use reaches a point of addiction—daily use—your brain may require a break to restore its default functioning. Your normal male instinct is stimulated by both visual and sensual stimuli, but if your brain is conditioned only to get stimulated visually, you risk complications to your sex life, such as porn-induced erectile dysfunction. Further, you will gradually learn to separate the physical release from the emotional connection. You will only engage in soulless sex. Your brain needs the real thing.

When it comes to addiction, I don't believe in self-discipline but environmental control. That is, decrease the chances of temptation by removing the seductive stimuli. How to achieve this goal is complex and beyond the scope of this book. However, I hope raising awareness of the issue and its potential ramifications opens the door to some changes in your environment so that your access to porn is not as instant and tempting.

Takeaway messages to activate your Lover

Your purpose as a Lover is to cultivate connection in your relationship. This connection will enable your family to flourish. Feeling connected is essential for the stability of your relationship and the well-being of your family. Connecting may not come naturally for you, particularly if you are very high in your Warrior energy. But if you activate your Lover energy, you give your wife the gift of your heart. The more you connect, the happier she will become.

Your action plan

- Always try to stay engaged.
- Keep her trust in you as something sacred. Avoid addictive behaviors that damage your reliability.
- Strengthen your relationship resilience by creating moments of connection, e.g., shared activities.
- Get to know everything about each other through a daily catch-up.
- Speak the language of the heart—authentically share your needs and feelings.
- Use the soft-start tool to ensure that a conversation on a sore issue starts softly.
- Touch her regularly throughout the day.
- Address sexual frustrations courageously. Don't suppress or deny them.

6

ACTIVATE YOUR MAGICIAN TO
TRANSFORM REACTIVITY

*"The Magician has the capacity to detach from events—
the chaos of the world—and draw on essential truths and
resources. He thinks clearly in times of crisis and enables us
to take a broader view of things. The Magician governs our
ability to observe internally and develop self-awareness."*

**— Robert Moore and Douglas Gillette, King, Warrior,
Magician, Lover**

Here is a brief reminder of the Magician identity card that I
described in more detail in Chapter Three.

My identity	I am the King's adviser, coach, influencer, researcher, problem-solver.
My purpose	To transform situations and people.
How I work	I observe, reflect, and examine things on deeper levels. I consult and influence people.

Her voice:

"I can get very emotional at times and even volatile. I am not always sure why. It could be due to my hormones, the kids, general anxiety, or many other things that I take to heart. When my cup of distress is getting full, I need to release some of it. I may even offload it on you. Please don't take it personally. I really don't mean to upset you. I need your understanding and presence during these times. I am in a fog, overwhelmed by my feelings and my racing mind. If you react, you are sucked into my vortex. I need you to stay grounded and not buy into it. Stay close to me but keep some distance from my emotional mess. Your clarity and centeredness will help me get back to myself faster.

Just hold me, don't rush to fix me or problem-solve. I need you to listen patiently without judgment. And don't identify with my pain. Stay clear of that. Allowing me the space to process my hurt and release it provides me with the greatest support. Just be that space for me, and I will do the rest. I need you in such moments to help me keep things in perspective."

The role of the Magician is a bit more complex to comprehend and activate than the other three roles. So let me start with a few illustrations:

- Scenario A:

  Your wife is upset, she just yelled at your daughter who is now crying.

Your reaction may sound like this: "Why can't you leave her alone?" or "You sound like your mother!"

However, your Magician reaction should sound like this: "Yeah, our girl can be really difficult to handle" or "I see that you need a little rest, let me deal with her"

- Scenario B:

Your wife complains that you neglect the family because you are too busy working.

Your reaction may sound like this: "Do you think I do that for fun? I work hard for you!"

But your Magician should sound like this: "What do you mean 'neglect'?" or "What would you like me to do more of?" or "Yeah, I know. It has been crazy at work lately. Things are going to change soon..."

- Scenario C:

During an argument, your wife uses negative language to criticize and attack you.

Your reaction may sound like this: "And who do you think you are?" or "And you always…" or "You never…"

Your Magician should sound like this: "You are using very hurtful language. I don't like it. I am going to take a little break. Let's continue later."

The Magician applies the power of his mind to resolve issues. He sees what's below the surface and understands processes on their deeper levels. He often sees what other people can't see. His insights lead to effective solutions and interventions. He goes to the core of a matter and offers solutions that are practical, long-term, and preventative. As an expert in **how** things operate, he is able to create transformations.

To transform a situation, person, or organization, Magicians observe first. They observe intently to access and examine the facts. Scientists are Magicians. We have seen them in action during the coronavirus pandemic. They studied the virus, invented a solution, and supported the Kings with decision-making. The scholars I mentioned in Chapter One are Magicians—they help us to guard truth and science from the cultural bug ideologists. The first humans who used tools and language to transform their lives were our earliest Magicians.

To observe and examine data objectively, a Magician must use perspective. The higher the perspective point, the better. To gain a good perspective, he needs to keep himself at some distance from the objects of his investigation, away from chaos and emotions. He needs to be non-attached.

His 'wand' is the clarity and focus of his mind. He is not lost in times of crisis or stress. His mind stays clear thanks to his unique ability to respond to events in a non-reactive and objective manner. He does not get carried away emotionally. His 'magic' results from his unique ability to consider perspectives— he can see reality through the 'clouds' and hear truth through the 'noise.'

To transform human emotions and behaviors, the Magician tries first to understand them. This is what we do in the science of psychology. We try to make sense of why people are the way they are so that we can help both them and society. As Magicians, psychologists expose our vulnerabilities, flaws, biases, irrationality, disorders, and more. This provides a good reason to dislike psychologists: they direct light into areas we would rather keep in the darkness. They act as 'bullshit detectors.' Who likes to look in such a mirror?!

Yet, the Nobel Prize committee recognized the importance of telling this unpleasant truth. In 2002, they gave the Nobel Prize to Daniel Kahneman, a cognitive psychologist who specializes in exposing people's errors of judgment and poor decisions. As a classic Magician, he shares his truth which challenges and changes us. His work is described in the book Thinking Fast and Slow. Wisdom will require us to slow down, he taught us. Our fast, automatic, and reactive system is our "lazy system." Most of the time, we operate from this system. We act spontaneously and impulsively without much consideration for outcomes. No wonder this quick system often leads to trouble!

On the other hand, the system of executive parts in our brain is slower. Our prefrontal cortex is responsible for planning and self-regulating. To activate it, we need to slow down. Kings and Magicians act slower. They take the time to learn about a situation and examine their options. This increases their chances of responding appropriately. Warriors by comparison must act swiftly. However, before Warriors can act effectively, they must slowly build their skills.

The *Moneyball* movie gives us a rare opportunity to see a Magician at work. It tells the true story of the extraordinary success of a baseball team. The club directors want to buy new players based on their aura and public image, but a young nerdy-looking guy simply suggests looking at players' stats before deciding whether to buy them. The data tells a different story about which players to buy, which challenges the authority of the directors. They get upset. Typically, they give the nerdy guy a hard time before setting aside their bias and consulting reality. When they finally did, the results were extraordinary.

Recall the 'noise' I mentioned in Chapter Four on the King. A King follows a system with clear rules and ignores the noise.

The Magician husband

As the Magician husband, you are reflective, not reactive. You approach family matters with the desire to understand and resolve, rather than to win or control. You listen and inquire. You experiment with solutions until you find what works. You are pragmatic. You don't get bogged down in arguments because you are interested in what works, rather than what is 'right'. Conflicts are not a threat to you, but opportunities to grow. You are open to learning because you don't take any drama personally. Instead of being defensive, you try to make sense of what is going on. With your curious mind, you ask questions and seek to understand. You remain stoic and endure the natural hardships and pains that come with the complex task of raising a family. Like other pains in life, you understand that they will pass.

You will need your Magician to deal wisely and calmly with the intense emotional reactivity that takes place daily in your family life.

Why are we so reactive?

Family is the birthplace of our emotional life. For better or worse, this is where we experience our deepest feelings. It is where we are most easily triggered. Just think about your parents and how you get reactive around them. Now that you are married, this reactivity has shifted to your wife. The closer people are to us, the more they matter to us and the stronger we feel towards them. And when we feel more 'at home', we relax our pretending and defending mechanisms. We express our emotional hurts more freely. Think of that child who is an 'angel' at school and a 'monster' at home. As someone once said, "family is the rubbish bin of our emotions."

Blame our attachment brain for our reactivity. It is the center of our socio-emotional instincts. We are triggered so deeply because our attachment brain is concerned with our survival. To survive, we need the closeness of other human beings. We need security and belonging. We want to know that there is at least one person in the world who we can rely on to care for us in times of need. When we finally find this person, they become not only a source of joy, but also of worry, frustration, and disappointment. We place a great deal of power in their hands. Their impact on us is immense. This is why you and your wife are naturally reactive towards each other. It is also why your conflicts can escalate so quickly and so dramatically. They provoke fear because your attachment brain interprets conflicts as threats of rejection and abandonment. Indeed, separation is a scary and painful experience.

Your attachment brain is automatic and reactive, leaving you with little choice. It makes you angry, defensive, argumentative, resistant, and avoidant. When you are so close to another person, your lens gets blurry. There is no space and no distance to allow for perspective and clarity. This is the nature of attachment.

The magic you want to create is that little space between action and reaction, between stimuli and response, between you and your bodily reactions. The magic is your ability to see things with clarity, examine them with curiosity, and find out what works. It's not easy to create this magic. Even top professionals struggle to do it with their own families.

You need the power of the Magician to help you transform your reactivity into balanced and level-headed responses. As one of my clients put it: "When I am more stoic, the relationship is better."

How reactivity damages
your marriage

Sadly, during hard times partners tend to blame each other too quickly. I suggest blaming reactivity instead. Just as we don't blame toddlers for throwing a tantrum, we shouldn't blame each other for our reactivity. We need to examine it and find ways to manage it more effectively. Let's start with getting to know the impacts of reactivity on any close relationship.

It escalates conflicts.

Reactivity locks partners in a cycle of action and reaction. The more you do 'A' (e.g., avoiding), the more she does 'B' (e.g., protesting), and vice versa. After hundreds of these times, conflicts only escalate because you both feel helpless with this deeply ingrained habit of reacting to each other. If such a cycle is left untreated for too long, the danger is that despair kicks in. You both give up and you distance yourself from each other. Detachment is looming.

It undermines order.

Everyone needs order to feel secure and stable. However, reactive emotions such as anger and anxiety stem from primitive parts of your brain that generate responses such as "fight or flight." You don't choose or control these responses. When they suddenly appear, you might feel impulsive, fragmented, and out of balance. And as your values and integrity are being compromised, the order in your family is damaged.

It is drawn to negative feelings.

Reactivity is designed for short-term survival. Nature wants you to be quick and automatic during times of danger. This is the purpose of feelings such as hurt, fear, and anger. They make you either avoid risk or fight to protect. They are 'negative' because they are unpleasant, but their purpose is survival. The more people are vulnerable in their survival, the more they focus on what's wrong. This is why children constantly complain to parents. Children are reactive. Since women, and mothers in particular, are generally more vulnerable and anxious than men, they also tend to be more reactive, on edge, and more prone to consider the worst.

It is personal.

Reactivity reflects our bias to take things personally even when they are not. The egoic mind makes itself super important, as if issues are all about ourselves. As if we are the cause of everything, good or bad.

For example, if your wife looks unhappy, you might wonder "What have I done wrong?" Or if you didn't call her from work today, she could wonder "Does he care about me?" Or if your child is upset, your wife may believe it's her fault. The female mechanism makes her prone to identify with others' pain. This makes your wife even more inclined to take things personally.

It makes you easy to manipulate.

Reactivity makes you lose power. You cannot operate as King or Warrior because you are out of balance and out of focus. You are vulnerable to your own urges, fears, and greed. You are at risk of applying bad judgment and being manipulated by others.

I have seen too many men being controlled by their wives like puppets on strings. She has access to the strings because men don't see and don't own their needs and feelings. When men are disconnected from their emotional selves, they are unaware of their needs. They leave a vacuum for someone else to take charge of them. They lose their autonomy. They are emasculated, but they don't even know it.

As you can see, reactivity is the main culprit in relationship troubles. You will need the power of your Magician to transform this reactivity.

Gender differences in reactivity

Feminine energy is shaped by ancient instincts of motherhood. Bonding with babies is not a choice for mothers but a hard-wired biological mechanism. Mothers are compelled to react when their babies are in distress. This physiological mechanism guarantees that the mother meets the baby's needs. A child's pain is a mother's pain.

This reactivity is a double-edged sword—it keeps babies alive, but also makes mothers vulnerable. A mother's strong identification with her child means that the well-being of your children has an enormous impact on your wife's mood. A mother is as vulnerable as her most vulnerable child. When it comes to your children, your wife is far more reactive than you and she needs your support and understanding. She may be on edge because the sound of a distressed child hits her at her core. Never underestimate the impact.

As a man, it is easier for you to maintain a degree of separation and distance from the emotional drama of parenting. For better or worse, the distress of a child affects you differently.

This has to do with the fact that you are not the one who carried the baby for 9 months in your body. Further, years of hunting and fighting have taught your male brain to exercise self-control if you are to succeed on your mission. If you get too scared or too excited, you may lose the 'battle.' Self-regulation and self-control are also mechanisms that help you to protect both yourself and others from the savage and destructive sides of your male brain. Renowned marriage researcher John Gottman captures this well: "Male's ability to self-soothe is critical if marriages are to survive."[71]

Research on emotional reactivity and down-regulation shows that there are some gender differences. Women tend to react more strongly to stressful events, resulting in a higher prevalence of female depression and anxiety. One study tried to dig deeper into the brain to assess gender differences in reactivity. Taking a whole-brain approach, the researchers used fMRI to assess how male and female brains differ in their reactions to unpleasant stimuli. They found a significantly greater regulation effect in men compared to women. The prefrontal brain responsible for the top-down process of down-regulation was more active in men. The researchers concluded that men might engage in more automatic, less deliberate processes than women when regulating emotions. Interestingly, those 'deliberate processes' refer to how women down-regulate negative emotions by creating positive ones.[72] Now you can understand why your wife may ask you to give her a hug or make her laugh.

This unique male capacity to down-regulate reactive emotions can serve you and your family well. This masculine strength is the stoic man at his best. The challenge of working effectively with reactive emotions will require you to go deeper into their unseen world—the feminine mystery world. As creatures of actions, solutions, and measurable results, men are predisposed to focus on external tasks rather than delving into this inner, subconscious world. Yet, this is the wonderland where personal growth takes place. You may need to go deeper into this world before you can go higher for a better perspective. Since this land is my workplace, I have a few insights and 'tricks' to share with you.

Becoming a Magician

A Magician uses the power of his mind, particularly the power of attention and intention. Attention is your psychic energy. It is precious and limited. Every single moment, there are so many stimuli from inside and outside your body fighting for your attention. You may struggle to keep focused with this ongoing bombardment of stimuli. But the one who controls your attention controls you, so it is better for you to control it yourself.

To master your attention, you use your intention. Intention has an organizing capacity and can lead your attention. Intention takes the form of your values, goals, plans, imagination, ideals, and expectations. In other words, the thoughts you project into the future. If you ever feel inspired by an idea or a book (such as this one hopefully), you sense how your attention is harnessed in a certain direction. For example, your intention to be a good husband is leading your attention towards this book.

With intention you are being proactive rather than reactive. You live out your sense of agency, leading, and mastering your future. Intention has the hypnotic power to mobilize the attention of both yourself and others. Interestingly, the medical meaning of intention is "the healing process of a wound."

Intentions and expectations are responsible for well-known placebo effects in medical research, and they are also responsible for 15% of the outcomes in counseling.[73] If you master your intention and attention, then you master the power of your mind. Ask yourself these questions:

- "Right now, what is my intention and where is my attention?
- "Are they aligned?"

Answering these questions requires you to use your mind rather than being used by it, as it happens most of the time.

Is there a way to learn how to use our mind?

Yes, we have a way to help us become masters of our minds, even if only for brief moments. It's called "mindfulness." Mindfulness has become a very popular tool used by millions around the world. It has been extensively researched and is now used in counseling. There are many courses and methods that can train you to develop the mindfulness skill, but for our purposes in this book, it suffices to discuss it briefly and explore how it works in the context of family life.

Mindfulness—the answer to reactivity

As the name implies, in a state of mindfulness your mind's capacity for intention and attention are being fully used. Your attention is aligned with your intention, with what you are focusing on right now. You are fully present and fully engaged in what you are doing.

Mindfulness is the art of directing your attention. Most of the time you are lost in your own thoughts, unaware of what you are doing or feeling. During mindfulness, you become the observer, the witness. You operate via your seeing and hearing senses. As a witness you take a temporary perspective of an 'outsider.' This non-attachment attitude is the unique power of the Magician in you.

Your reactive brain is ruled by biological mechanisms beyond your immediate control. You don't choose those mental and physiological events within you. Memories, images, thoughts, and body sensations appear involuntarily. But something miraculous happens the moment you observe them. As you are reading these words, be aware for a moment of any tension in your neck. What do you sense? Mindfulness of your body sensation results in a calming effect. The same effect will happen if you notice your breathing for a few seconds. You tend to slow down.

There are a few reasons for this calming effect. First, your body lives in the present moment only. Your mind may wander to the past and future, but your body always remains here and now. When you bring attention to your body, you connect with the present moment.

Second, awareness is an act of sensing and perceiving, which is less energy-consuming than analyzing, comprehending, or thinking. You direct your attention away from your effortful thinking brain to the effortless act of noticing.

Third, mindfulness is a relational skill. Awareness of your body soothes you much like your parents' attention did when you were a baby. You feel held. Attention to sensations in your body is an act of self-love. No wonder it has a soothing effect.

You need mindfulness—your capacity to observe—when your **reactivity is getting in the way**. Your defensiveness, withdrawal, and anger are signs of your mind interfering with your reality. Your Magician helps you to distinguish between parts and the whole, between beliefs and who you really are, and between mind-made stories and what is here and now. Each time you witness your mental-emotional reactive patterns, you take another small step towards liberating yourself from their grip.

Nature makes you grow up, and your Magician makes you wake up.

Being mindful of yourself

It is essential for a Magician to know and understand himself first before he can understand and help others. This was the top lesson the Greek philosophers taught many years ago—"Know thyself." It is the most famous personal growth lesson in history. This is where your wisdom begins.

Being aware of an underlying issue is the first big step towards healing. Once you recognize a dysfunctional pattern of thinking and feeling (and how it works), you are no longer at the mercy of its hidden forces. With knowledge and understanding of your vulnerabilities—such as worry, shame, anger, and helplessness—you gain some level of freedom. As you learn to relate to these feelings with acceptance, you are less likely to react and regret it later.

Obviously, we don't change our behaviors so easily. Some patterns are deeply ingrained. But the first step is to take the torch and start looking into the basement of our minds. As you can imagine, the things we keep in our basements are not the nicest. The 'mirror' is pretty ugly at times. We often don't like what we see. We think it's better to suppress, deny, or distort reality to make ourselves look nicer in the mirror.

A Magician does the opposite—he watches instead. He examines everything with the intention of knowing and understanding. In her book The Hero Within, Pearson says "What differentiates Magicians from others is their capacity for honest self-reflection. They neither shrink from seeing negative truth about themselves nor banish aspects of themselves that seem troubling. Rather, they seek to find the gold in the shadow."[74]

And this brings us to the golden rule of the Magician:

Transformation begins with seeing and accepting vulnerabilities.

It takes courage to look at our vulnerabilities to see what's beyond our defenses and pretenses. Courage is associated with action, but with mindfulness your courage is in how you acknowledge, see, and accept. Mindfulness implies an attitude of 'yes' towards your thoughts or feelings. Vulnerabilities such as stress, sadness, hurt, worry, and powerlessness need a different type of attention from you to see and accept them for what they are. Not to resist them. Not to deny them. Not to judge them. Not to control them. Vulnerabilities reflect our inner child, and this inner child needs an attitude of loving kindness from us. In his book *The Mindful Brain*, Dan Siegel put it this way: "Mindfulness can be seen as a way of developing a secure attachment with yourself."[75]

When you recognize, accept, and connect mindfully with vulnerable thoughts, feelings, or experiences, you start the process of healing them. It is a paradoxical process. Try to resist or suppress them, and you create more anger and tension in your body. Your reactivity gets worse. Think about angry parents as an example. Their anger reflects their struggle with a state of powerlessness. They are not angry with their child, but with not knowing what to do. Effective parents on the other hand rarely get angry. They simply enforce consequences.

Vulnerability is a primal and natural human experience. Your anger in most cases will mean reacting to your vulnerabilities as if they are threats to you. However, through mindfulness you will realize that these vulnerabilities are your allies, not your enemies. They are storytellers. Listen to them because they carry valuable information for you. For example, sadness tells you that you are letting go of an important loss, worry tells you about a threat to something important to you, and shame tells you that your inner critic is overactive. Powerlessness tells you that you need some tools or to restore power. In a non-reactive, mindful state you can slow down, listen, and allow your inner wisdom to guide you to the most appropriate response.

Self-acceptance is where your growth begins. It leads to you being more at peace with yourself first, and later at peace with others.

The impact of mindfulness

Mindfulness liberates you from the grip of your reactive, impulsive, and fragmented mind. It empowers you to make choices rather than be the victim of your fleeting urges and emotions. You are more free to lead your life according to your (King) values. And when you can make choices, you are more flexible and adaptable. This is a hallmark of mental health.

Mindfulness also enables you to build your capacity for empathy towards your own unpleasant experiences and those of your family members. Your feelings and thoughts are always okay as they are. They represent your inner child. Being mindful means to accept and understand them before you act on them. (One of my clients called his formula "My triple-A—Aware,

Acknowledge, and Accept.") Through empathy you come to see and embrace yourself and those you love. It enhances your connection and helps you to overcome self-doubt, inadequacy, judgment, and shame. The effect is not only less conflict, but more expression and authenticity.

Mindfulness also means being open to learning. Rather than deflect or defend, you remain open to feedback, which means a great deal for your wife. This will make her feel like she matters to you, and she will feel hope that she has some power to influence you. Research shows that a man's ability to accept influence from his wife is crucial for marriage success.[76]

While your internal experiences are involuntary, this is not the case with your behavior. You do have control over your words and actions, and you are held accountable for them. If you get into trouble for your behavior time and again, it is a sign of poor connection with your internal experiences. They manage you rather than you managing them. You fail to accept the lessons that life is trying to teach you. There is no learning.

But as you pay close attention and try to make sense of feelings such as anger, fear, and grief, you begin to learn what they are trying to teach you. From an evolutionary perspective, they carry important messages that are supposed to serve you. (This is why I prefer to call them 'unpleasant' rather than 'negative' feelings—they often have positive teaching value.) Listen to and investigate unpleasant feelings before reacting to them. Your internal therapist can help you with egoic tendencies such as resistance, stubbornness, rigidity, and defensiveness. Mindfulness and self-understanding will help you heal and grow.

And now to the greatest gift mindfulness can bring to your life—inner peace. When you **accept** your vulnerabilities and pains as they are without resistance, denial, or numbing, there is no internal battle anymore. And more peace means that new psychic energy becomes available to help you focus on your tasks.

"I zoom out my lenses"

James has been learning with me the art of observing his reactivity. After a while he started to appear calmer. His responses during family conflicts were not as aggressive. I asked what had worked for him. "I zoom out," he replied. The skill of observing his reactivity from above allowed him to see it as happening there, not here. That perspective changed everything for him.

The power of now

When I help my clients to cultivate their mindfulness capacity, I take inspiration from Eckhart Tolle, a luminary author and speaker. In his book The Power of Now, Tolle explains how mindfulness frees you from the suffering you inflict on yourself and others when your "mind-made little me" runs your life.[77] Your mind-made self results from your attachment to certain beliefs, and mindfulness is about freedom from these attachments. Any dogma, ideology, religion, or political belief that you identify with is located at the level of your mind-made self. You can tell by how easily you get triggered by these beliefs. You take them personally. The 'power of now' is the power of awareness. It is your capacity to observe what is going on in both your mind and body in the present moment.

In his books and talks, Tolle guides his audience to connect with their states of self-awareness. His unique style has made him one of the most popular speakers in the world. I encourage you to read his book and listen to his YouTube channel. (Note the viewers' comments!) Oprah Winfrey created a fantastic podcast called: Eckhart Tolle: Essential Teachings. Look it up; it's free. Tolle will empower your Magician capacity.

The three Magician levels

A Magician can see what other people don't see. Sometimes he is called a 'see-er.' In the context of our *Good Husband* project, the object you want to see is your mind—those hidden forces that drive your emotions and behaviors. The deeper and clearer you can see them, the better you can manage your reactivity. As a witness, you take the temporary perspective of an 'outsider.' You are non-attached. With each observation, you climb up the ladder towards a higher perspective. This perspective enables you to react less and reflect more. It is liberating.

Beginner Magician: name feelings

At this basic level, you will have the capacity to recognize and label your unpleasant feelings. Naming is a process of awareness. After all, to name a feeling you need to notice the body sensations it generates. Noticing it means you are in a relationship with the feeling rather than being caught up in it. Naming a feeling is a non-reactive intervention. For a split second, you are a witness to it. You are aware. This brief moment of awareness and naming of your body sensations will have a calming effect on you. The ancient wisdom of noticing and naming feelings has now become the modern science of mindfulness. Instead of operating via the reactive limbic system in your brain, you operate in the reflective prefrontal cortex, where you can regulate your body. Each time you are mindful of a body sensation, you strengthen your mindfulness muscle—your Magician.

To put your feelings into words, it is essential to have emotional literacy. Common feelings among family members include:

- feeling sad in reaction to a loss of connection or loneliness, or if your loved ones are in pain.
- feeling worried if your partner feels hurt or unwell.
- feeling anxious if a marital conflict is not repaired soon enough.
- feeling hurt when you are treated unkindly.
- feeling ashamed if you are blamed or judged.
- feeling disappointed when something you hoped and expected didn't happen.
- feeling rejected if your bid for connection is refused.
- feeling frustrated and powerless when your needs are not met.
- feeling fear if your partner makes threats or acts aggressively.

Men rarely share these feelings. Why? Because these feelings expose vulnerability and they make them feel uncomfortable. Instead, men tend to react with anger or withdrawal.

Earlier in the book we defined 'power' as your ability to influence. How well does anger or avoidance work for you? You lose power when you get angry with your wife or withdraw from her. Not only do you decrease the chance of her responding to you, but you also lose connection with her.

Men often ask me: "Don't I sound too weak and feminine with this talk of 'feelings'?" Well, you are weak when you use methods that defeat your goals and interests. You are strong if you express your feelings and needs in ways that bring your partner closer to you. This is power because your needs are more likely to be met.

Talking about vulnerability requires self-awareness and risk-taking. You first identify and name the feeling and then you share it before reactivity takes over. Acknowledging feelings is a process of empathy towards both yourself and your family members. You can make generic statements such as "It made me feel bad," "I am not comfortable with it," or "I didn't like it." Or you can be more specific with statements such as "It disappointed me," "I felt sad when…," or "It worries me that..."

Emotional literacy is not only crucial to your Magician role. It is also crucial to expressing your three other roles as King, Lover, and Warrior. And as you master this language, you are ready to move up to the next Magician level.

Advanced Magician: awareness of the 'filter' that generates feelings

At this level, you can see the deeper causes of feelings. You can recognize the filter in your mind that so often serves as the engine of your reactivity. I use the word 'filter' to describe a brain mechanism that interprets and perceives messages in a unique way. It's a kind of 'data processor' in your brain. Your response is not because 'A' happened, but because of the way your filter processed 'A.' Your filter makes the meaning—the 'narrative'—that you attach to the events in your life. What is a threat for one person is an opportunity for another; what is a failure for one is growth for another, and so forth.

Your unique filter reflects your personality and it dictates to a large degree how you absorb and digest experiences in your life. Messages don't land on a blank slate, but on a conditioned filter that consists of your memories, beliefs, and expectations. In marriage, your filter is ruled by your attachment brain. This brain mechanism makes you seek security with that one person you rely on to be there for you in times of need. Your attachment patterns are shaped by your personality and your history with caretakers. These patterns explain the way your filter operates in marriage.

In my clinic I have observed that male and female filters differ in their core themes. Women tend to interpret unpleasant interactions as signs of a loss of care and love, resulting in feelings of rejection and isolation. Men tend to interpret those moments as signs of failure, resulting in feelings of inadequacy and shame. Both genders react with a sense of powerlessness and anger.

The following tables highlight common differences between male and female filters.

Male filter examples

Event	Filter	Reaction
She looks upset.	"What have I done wrong?!"	Shame, defensiveness.
She bought something expensive.	"Such a waste… We won't have enough for other things."	Worry, stress.
She says "I am exhausted" in bed.	"She is not interested in having sex with me."	Rejection, resentment.
Conflict.	"I am weak, I don't know how to help here."	Shame, fear.

Female filter examples

Event	Filter	Reaction
He stays longer at work.	"I am alone. He avoids me."	Sadness, resentment.
He raised his voice.	"This is dangerous."	Fear
He doesn't help with the kids.	"I do everything here. This is not fair."	Indignation, anger.
Conflict.	"I can't get through to him."	Helplessness, powerlessness.

Your filter is so ingrained in your brain that you are unaware it's working on you. It has become your identity. That is, you identify with the content of your filter—your beliefs about yourself and others. These beliefs become the truth of who you are. Without a proper perspective, you get reactive and emotional due to your filter, as if you live inside a movie. You need to find a way out of the 'screen' and into a place where you can 'zoom out' and observe. This is a process of becoming aware of your hidden assumptions and beliefs. If you attend counseling, this is the biggest benefit you get—seeing and understanding these hidden forces that operate on you. As an advanced Magician, you become your own therapist—cultivating self-awareness and self-knowing.

Since your filters are often the source of pain for both of you, the 'magic' you are seeking is to create some differentiation between you and your filter. You want to loosen its grip on you. The problem is not in beliefs such as "I am inadequate" or "I am a failure," but your relationship with those beliefs. You hold them so tightly that there is no room for 'space'—a healthy distance that allows perspective and examination. Mindfulness of your filter will give you the space you need to avoid being reactive.

Take a look at these statements:

A. I am inadequate.

B. My mind is saying "I am inadequate."

A. I will never get it right.

B. I notice the belief that "I will never get it right."

A. She is trying to hurt me.

B. I am aware of the thought that "She is trying to hurt me."

What is the difference between each pair of 'A' and 'B' statements? Can you sense the different impact?

In the 'A' statements, the beliefs are experienced as truths. The 'B' statements represent awareness of these beliefs and are always true!

Right now the truth is not the story in your mind, but the fact that there are some appearances in your mind and you are noticing them. As an advanced-level Magician you can see your thoughts for what they are, and as you hold them more lightly, you enable self-humor and self-empathy.

As you are reading about your filter, you are beginning to develop a relationship with your automatic mind. This relationship means there is **You,** and there is **It**. You have created a little distance between you and your conditioned mind. As you loosen its grip on you, your beliefs are held lightly, not tightly. A little magic happens in the space you create between stimuli and response. In this tiny space lies your freedom to choose, and your ability to reflect before you react.

Reflection may sound like wondering: "Is that so?" "What do you mean?" or "What makes you assume that?" Such questions draw attention to your filter—your interpreter. They help with reality checks.

Once you have won a little freedom as an advanced Magician, you want to make the best use of it. This is the level of the expert Magician.

Expert Magician: switch from 'red' to 'green' filter

At this level, you have the capacity not only to be aware of your filter but to transform it. And the one who can master his filter also masters his feelings and general well-being. It is a bit of a lofty and complex idea to accomplish, but I include it here anyway in case you wish to stretch yourself.

Imagine you are driving between two landscapes. On the right-hand side, you see dry, barren, and rocky land. Among the rocks, people are hiding and occasionally shooting bullets towards the road. On the left-hand side, you see a lush and colorful landscape. It's very appealing. But where will your attention go most of the time? To the side from where bullets are coming. Your intention to survive is far greater than your intention for personal growth and leisure.

This metaphor illustrates the tension between two types of filters in our mind: one is ruled by the intention for short-term survival. I call it the "red filter." The other is ruled by the intention for long-term growth. I call it the "green filter."

Your red filter will focus your attention on danger and risks. It is quick, automatic, and 'negative.' It is a relic in our brain from when humans needed to stay vigilant to survive in the wilderness. Our red filter is more active when we move into the unknown or deal with uncertain situations. When raising children, this red filter will be particularly strong in your wife.

Your green filter will draw your attention towards possibilities, opportunities, and the 'positive.' This green filter creates optimism bias—we approach situations with too much hope and too little caution. Pollyanna syndrome is a good example. It is the tendency to be too optimistic and positive while denying risks and flaws. Falling in love is another bias of the green filter. We magnify the positive sides of the person so that our dreams will come true.

Watch a toddler and see the earliest interplay between these two filters during the attachment phase. One moment he wants to be close to his parents so he can feel secure, and another moment he moves away to explore and learn. The toddler continually moves between the desire for survival-security, and the desire for adventure-growth.

Our challenge is to be aware of how these two filters play in our brain and master them to our advantage. For survival reasons, the bias to see risks via our red filter is far more common. In the context of marriage, this red filter causes a great deal of misunderstanding and conflict because partners interpret each other via the lens of survival in their attachment brain. The expert Magician is aware of this subconscious process and considers "green" interpretations instead. Take for example the scarcity mindset, when a person focuses on what they don't have, what's wrong, etc. (i.e., uses the red filter). To rectify a scarcity mindset, cultivate an abundance mindset of gratitude and appreciation instead (i.e., use your green filter). If your partner tends to spend too much time criticizing and complaining, this is an obvious red filter 'bug.' To rectify it, you shouldn't defend or argue, but ask her what she needs or wants from you.

People who regularly use their red filter tend to make two cognitive mistakes. Firstly, they **personalize**. They regard the message or behavior as being aimed at them personally. They fail to consider other intentions or motivations. Secondly, they **generalize**. They make the event something global and pervasive. They often talk in terms of "always" and "never" and fail to see the context of the situation. So when you or your partner talks like that, remember that it's the red filter speaking.

Let's look at some strategies to buffer against that filter and transform reactivity.

THE MAGICIAN IN ACTION

The following tools will help you activate your Magician and transform reactivity:

- mindful tools,
- externalize your filter,
- heal your shame,
- transform your emotional flooding,
- empathize with your wife,
- Coach her to start softly,
- prime for positivity,
- deal effectively with victimhood, and
- influence with written messages.

Let's look at each tool in more detail.

Mindful tools

Notice - As you are reading now, notice any tension in your neck for a moment. If you do, you will see the immediate impact of noticing the sensation. This is the magic of mindfulness. The very act of paying attention to your body's sensation will cause it to change.

Do the same with your breathing. The mere act of noticing it will slow your breathing down and create a sense of calmness. When you do the same process with another person, we call it empathy. As you notice and validate their feelings, their body responds with calmness. They have been 'seen.'

Now you can see the strong link between mindfulness and empathy, and between empathy and stress reduction.

To speak mindfully to your partner, begin your sentences with 'noticing' words such as "I see...," "I hear...," or "I sense...." These words are descriptive, not evaluative. They are free from any judgment, analysis, or interpretations. In your Magician role, you examine data with the curiosity of a scientist. You reflect, rather than react.

Name feelings - As explained earlier, naming feelings is the beginner level in the Magician academy. To recognize and name a body sensation is to begin the process of regulating it. Clinical experience and brain research provide robust evidence on how naming feelings can help to regulate them.[78] Words in this case can do magic. We need to name feelings, particularly when they are very unpleasant. To use terms such as "worried," "angry," "sad," or "hurt" to describe your feelings does **not** mean that you are negative.

Naming unpleasant feelings helps to calm them down, as in the saying "name it to tame it." It means you are tending to them. Notice the impact on your child when you say something like "I see you are feeling angry / sad / afraid."

Naming feelings is a challenge for many people, but I hope you can see why emotional literacy is an essential part of the magic. A man who struggles to describe his feelings often experiences frustration and powerlessness because his partner won't understand him. Further, his partner might feel the same when her feelings are not validated.

Accept - The instinct of many men is to treat their emotions with control strategies such as suppressing, resisting, judging, and numbing them. They say "no" to their bodies. They try to fight or numb their vulnerabilities. Some may resort to substances to help with this numbing, while others may invest in building ever stronger muscles.

But fighting emotions is like fighting the waves when your boat is shaking. We need to work **with** them, not against them. The paradox of our hurts is that in order to diminish them, they need to be accepted and validated. The saying "what you resist persists" is very true here.

Your internal experiences of thoughts and feelings are spontaneous. You don't choose them. Therefore, judging them as right or wrong is no point. They just 'are.' Wise mothers realize this truth when they hold their crying babies rather than getting stressed and trying to control the crying. The child inside you craves a similar unconditional acceptance and presence. This is the true meaning of self-love. *Beauty and the Beast* conveys the same idea—to change the beast, you first accept it as it is.

Be curious - Being open and curious is a scientist at his best. Your body reacts with tension, but your Magician wants to inquire first, just in case you didn't get it right. "What is it? What is going on here? What does it mean?" You want to know what is behind the words. This curiosity tool helps you get the facts to make sense of a situation. It is your ultimate antidote to defensiveness. Imagine your wife saying something like "You don't care about me," or "You never help," and you reply with "What do you mean?" This is a classic Magician's reply—you have just cut the fuse of a 'bomb.'

Use humor - When stand-up comedians laugh at themselves, we all laugh with them because we enjoy the comic perspective on weird thoughts, feelings, or habits. We relate to these experiences and it's fun to see them 'there' in person on stage. Distance enables our laughter. Looking at our involuntary thoughts and feelings through the lens of humor is a wonderful way to create perspective. You disidentify with them. You loosen their grip on your ego. They are no longer personal, and you can be a bit more amused by what you discover inside your busy brain. Self-deprecating humor is your antidote to your serious and self-important ego.

Respond slowly - Reacting is automatic and fast. Responding involves more care and thoughtfulness. As you apply your Magician, you slow down your responses. This is when awareness becomes crucial. You are first aware of the tension growing in your body, then interpret it as a sign to slow down. In his classic book *Thinking, Fast and Slow,* Daniel Kahneman describes two systems in our brain: one is fast, automatic, intuitive, and impressionable; the other is slow, reflective, and thoughtful. His research on decision-making demonstrates how relying on your quick, impulsive system often leads to mistakes and bad outcomes.

You need to slow down to avoid reactive behaviors and their negative consequences. This allows for deeper understanding, careful consideration, and reasonable, more effective interventions. The paradox of this magic is that to get to the solution faster, you need to slow down.[79]

PRACTICE:

Share this list of these non-reactive tools of mindfulness with your partner and discuss which are the most usable for you. Try to rank them from top to bottom, and then take it upon yourself to practice the two that are most useful for you.

Externalize your filter

Too often people see a thinking pattern as part of their identity. They tend to personalize it so that it becomes part of who they are—for example, "I am inadequate," "I am a failure," or "I am worthless." They fail to see the difference between who they really are and their mind-made filter. The impact is a sense of hopelessness, helplessness, and toxic shame. To help you loosen the grip of certain debilitating beliefs, we use the tool of externalization.

Externalization helps you to create a unique perspective on a 'mental bug.' I call it a 'mental bug' because it is unnoticeable and affects your mind just like a virus affects your body. Similar to a virus, we will put this mental bug under a 'microscope' to learn how it operates.

However, unlike vaccinations for viruses, the 'vaccination' for a mental bug happens during the process of examination. Learning the mechanism of the bug is how you liberate yourself from its impact. Any moment of looking at it is a moment of differentiation. There is you, and there **it**—the mental bug—is.

In your dark basement, a bug makes a lot of noise. But like gremlins, your bug can't stand light. So you take it out and bring it into the 'light' of your awareness. You examine it with the curiosity of a scientist. The more time you spend assessing and observing it, the more you will see it as separate from you. One of my clients jokingly summed it up this way: "I got it; you did an exorcism on me! It works; the evil spirit no longer has a hold on me..."

Indeed, humor is one of the immediate effects of externalization. Stand-up comedians make use of that when they laugh at their issues. We laugh with them because it is liberating to observe and share our 'evil spirits.'

The healing occurs because you gradually come to see the bug as not who you are, but just a part of you. It wants to hold a big space, but you make it smaller. "Ah, I recognize you, you little bugger," you smile at it.

The same principle applies to how you help your wife and children cope with their mental bugs. We all have them! Let's assume that your wife gets very angry in certain situations, and you both have acknowledged her vulnerability. A gentle statement such as "I am afraid it is your pain speaking now" may remind you both that she is in the grip of her mental bug. It will allow more understanding and prevent escalation.

Externalization not only helps you to develop more astute awareness of your reactivity, but it also helps you to consolidate your identity as the **aware one** and as the witness, not as the problem. You are who you are, and the problem is the problem. The essence of who you are is **not** the content of your mind. This realization is a Magician at his best.

PRACTICE:

Reflect on situations in which you frequently feel reactive. Investigate the trigger and its impact on you. Examine it and recognize it as your mental bug that attacks you from time to time. To treat it with some humor and lightness, choose a cute name for it. The following tool for healing shame will give you some ideas.

Heal your shame

Throughout this book, you learn about your wife's core mental bug—her anxiety and her primary need to feel secure and safe. It's now time to reflect on men's core vulnerability—shame. (Obviously, women also suffer from shame and men also suffer from anxiety, but different biological and evolutionary forces drive their primal needs and desires.)

As a 'do-er' and performer, your primary desire is to express your potential, talents, and skills. This is your power, but also your vulnerability. That's because if you are not meeting certain standards and expectations, then you are at some risk of losing love. These are the two engines of shame:

1. the social standards that appear in your head as the voices of 'should' and 'shouldn't.'
2. the threat of losing love and belonging if you don't live up to the standards.

While guilt refers to a specific behavior for which we can say sorry, shame is about your being not doing. It is about who you are as a person and how worthy of love you are. Condemnation and criticism question how lovable you are. It is so painful because it hurts you at your core.

Condemnation comes both from within yourself and from

others. From within, your inner critic haunts you with a barrage of self-doubt and criticism. Externally, you are judged and blamed for not doing enough or doing things incorrectly. Since boys tend to test boundaries, go wild and defy authority more than girls, they receive more condemnation and criticism for their behavior. Their educators from an early age are usually women who are confronted by their boyish and hyperactive behaviors. The result is constant reprimanding, which makes boys feel bad about themselves. In recent years, we have witnessed the impact of a new player—the cultural bug. Men and masculinity are even more exposed to the trend of condemning and shaming. From an evolutionary perspective, we see a balancing act: women use their verbal strength to balance males' physical strength. You have the capability to make your wife feel scared, while she has the capability to make you feel ashamed.

Acting and performing are expressions of male sexuality. To fulfill our sexual energy, we need to pursue, chase, conquer, penetrate, and ejaculate. That's quite a few tasks and barriers to cross before our mission is accomplished. That's quite a few tasks and barriers to cross before our mission is accomplished. Furthermore, men's sexual energy is such an essential part of their psyche but is so poorly understood and treated by society. A man is exposed to constant sexual stimuli, which generate sexual tension in his body and a desire to act. Yet, he must hold himself together and can hardly discuss it with anyone. Releasing this energy is his big secret. Male time spent on porn sites is not considered by society to be equivalent to female time spent on social media. So men tend to go underground and hide their sexual preoccupation.

And hiding is how shame works. It makes you pretend, cover, and mask.

For healing, we need to bring the bug of shame into the light and examine it. Over the years, my clients have given this bug various names: Elliot the dragon ("for the fire it shoots at me"), Wombat ("for how it digs under the ground and creates damage below the surface"), Cloud ("for how it blurs my thinking"), and Torpi ("it acts like a torpedo on me, it makes me sink"). Here are some typical answers during inquiry into the mental bug of shame.

- How does it think?

  I am not enough, I am inadequate, I am a fraud, an imposter.

  I am not worthy of love because I don't live up to the standards.

  I don't belong here. I am flawed and unworthy of love.

  I constantly need to prove myself.

- What's its motto?

  I am not lovable as I am.

- How does it make you feel?

  A mix of dread, anger, sadness, and self-loathing.

  My body curls up.

  I want to disappear.

  I am alone with my secrets.

- What are some of its long-term effects?

  Isolation.

  Loss of joy.

  Constant tension.

An internal battle with my demons.

Nagging self-doubts.

Depression.

- How does it affect your relationship?
  It blocks connection.
  It makes me angry and defensive.
  I withdraw.

- How does it affect your career?
  I am critical and judgmental towards myself and others.
  A loss of motivation.
  Damaged working relationships.
  Reduced productivity.

- What does it make you do?
  I may try to escape it by various addictive habits.
  I avoid social situations that may provoke the bug.

- What makes it stronger?
  When I get feedback that puts doubts on how worthy I am.
  When I behave in ways that don't reflect my values.

- If the bug loosens its grip on you, what possibilities open up for you?
  Inner peace.
  Joy.
  Connection.

- What does the shame bug want from you?
  What's its purpose?
  It wants to keep me on track, to motivate me to work harder, to stay loyal to my values.

As you can see, the shame bug's intention is actually good! Like an autoimmune disease, it mistakenly attacks you. It attacks your psyche while trying to motivate you to behave in ways that keep peace in your heart. Similarly, your wife's anxiety bug also has good intentions—to help keep her safe and secure.

Three antidotes to the shame bug

Shame goes to the core of our being. It is about who you are and your worthiness. By comparison, guilt is about what you have done. You may say sorry and be forgiven for your guilt. The pain is deeper with shame, and coping with it is more complex. You heal shame through experiences of understanding, acceptance, and empathy. This is what you would hope to experience with a good partner, friend, or psychotherapist.

1. Recognizing it

I cannot stress enough how urgent and important it is to be aware of the shame bug. Shame researcher Brené Brown coined the term "shame resilience" to describe the strategies people use to combat the shame bug. She explains that awareness is your very first step. You want to recognize and call it shame. Your body may cringe, but you will say to your wife "This is shaming, and I don't appreciate it. Please never speak to me like that."

Your main challenge is to call out shaming. This is so hard because the very nature of shame is to cover and hide. It doesn't want to be seen. People in a state of shame are often not even aware that they are feeling it. They react by pretending or avoiding. Their shame story is told via their body language—a sunken posture and face covering.

2. Accepting it

Your shame may not be pleasant to you, but it needs a different response than resistance or avoidance. Battling it only creates more tension. Like a cat with its tail on fire, running away from shame only makes matters worse. Your emotional hurts need a 'yes' attitude from you, similar to what the baby inside you needed years ago—unconditional acceptance. To help heal shame, you should move towards it, not away from it. Your hurts want to be seen, validated, and embraced by you. When you share them with people who are capable of having empathy towards you, the experience of healing can be profound.

In a state of self-acceptance, you realize that:

- it's okay to change your mind,
- it's okay to make mistakes,
- it's okay to say I don't know,
- it's okay to be vulnerable, and
- it's even okay to fail.

3. Appreciating yourself

As a 'do-er,' you want to be acknowledged and appreciated for your actions. After all this is what mattered to her the most when she chose you to be her husband. Your status and achievements likely resulted from your hard work. However, if you are both coping with the challenge of raising children, then there is a risk that your efforts are not being appreciated. This is likely to be because your wife is overwhelmed by parenting tasks and her own self-doubts. Instead of words of appreciation, you may hear complaints and criticism.

During couples therapy, some men get teary when their partner shares her appreciation. These tears represent a deep longing to experience acknowledgment. Words of appreciation or admiration do you good in the same way that your support and connection help your wife feel loved and secure.

When gay people felt they had enough of hiding, they launched the "pride parade." No more shame, but pride instead. Not covering, but exposing. Not going in, but coming out.

These parades celebrate authenticity and hold a healing message for all of us—I am okay as I am. We are lovable as we are.

Similarly, you want to feel lovable as you are, not for what you do. When bad actions lead to bad consequences, it is the law of life. It's not personal. Life teaches lessons and you just need to be a good student. Take the lessons and grow.

"Loveable as I am"

Tom came to see me after a painful fight with his wife of 15 years. She blamed him for showing no care towards her and for being selfish. She threatened him with divorce. He felt hurt and helpless, and he withdrew further into himself.

Her complaints triggered his shame. He felt like a failure and only wanted to make the walls of his fortress thicker.

I encouraged him to treat his internal experiences with unconditional love—notice, accept, embrace, be together. I then invited him to close his eyes and quietly repeat the sentence "I am lovable as I am."

Tears came down his face. His walls dissolved for a moment. He allowed himself to yearn and to be vulnerable.

When he later shared the experience with his partner, she related to him differently. She connected to his pain and understood his need to feel accepted. She felt closer to him.

Transform your emotional flooding

As a 'do-er,' you experience your power through fixing problems. You may be able to fix problems at work, but family problems are often not as easily fixed. You may try really hard, only to realize how powerless you are. This powerlessness exposes vulnerability If you argue, your frustration may grow even bigger when your wife outsmarts you with her superior verbal skills. You may feel humiliated and lost for words. Tension will grow in your body and you may feel like you are about to explode. This is the point of emotional flooding.

Emotional flooding is more common among men. Women typically describe it with statements like "In a few seconds, he jumps from zero to 180 km/h," or "Suddenly, he explodes with rage." Flooding is a call for you to be mindful. Tension was building up in your body before the explosion and you were not aware of it! Recall the 'noticing' and 'naming' tools, and explore what has provoked your tension. Recognize that your body has released the stress hormone. It means you have reacted to a threat. Your body has activated the "fight or flight" reaction.

In a state of flooding, there is 'no one home.' The Magician has already lost. The magic is in **preparing** for your next round. You are wise when you equip yourself with mindfulness tools to respond as soon as you notice the first signs of physiological arousal in your body.

For a start, treat this flooding as a psychological bug that attacks you. Reflect with curiosity about the threat and consider support from a friend or professional. Is it the threat of losing your wife? Or being shamed by her? Or losing power and exposing your vulnerabilities? Are you being triggered by past experiences of powerlessness?

Self-understanding and self-empathy can help to reduce your tension, but they won't remove it altogether. You need to have a constructive 'valve' for releasing your tension. Women don't often reach the point of flooding because they release their tensions through talking and crying. However, boys and men tend to use their hands rather than words—slamming doors, punching, or throwing something.

Obviously, these temporary relief valves are not your winning strategies. They damage trust and scar your relationship. Recall the female sensitivity to anything that provokes anxiety. Acting out your frustrations may scare your wife so badly that she experiences it as a micro betrayal. Therefore, it's crucial and urgent for you to find a constructive way to express your emotional flooding.

To counter the "fight or flight" reaction, you can stimulate your vagus nerve (Google it!). This longest nerve in our body operates our parasympathetic system which specializes in resting and digesting. Scientists have found that we can increase our "vagal tone" (i.e., stimulate this nerve) by using simple strategies such as breathing slower, humming, laughing, and… speaking![80]

Verbal expression is your best way to transform reactive flooding. This is when emotional literacy becomes essential. Saying words such as "I am hurt / frustrated / disappointed / sad / disrespected / worried" gives you power! You are not helpless anymore. Instead, you have noticed what's happening and made your wife aware of your feelings. In a flooding state you may say statements like "I am so furious with…," "This is shocking for me," "I am so pissed off with that," "This is horrible," "You have got me really mad now," "You are killing me with your comments," etc.

But words alone may not be enough to soothe you during your emotional flooding. You may need an emergency valve. It is sometimes best to call for a little break and move away from each other. Tell her something like "I need a little break here to breathe," or "I am going to lose it; we better stop now." You should commit to completing the conversation and be clear about when that will happen. Always add something like "I will get back to the topic after dinner." Your withdrawal makes matters worse if your wife interprets it as avoiding or rejecting her. Constructive verbal expression is the alternative to the other two destructive ways of dealing with emotional flooding—suppression and aggression.

I don't support 'anger management' programs because I find them insulting to men. We tell men to deal with the symptom, namely aggression, only because it worries us. We wouldn't care about these men if it was not for their aggression. To show true care we need to help men deal with the causes of their anger—feelings such as hurt, shame, humiliation, grief, fear, or past brutalization and trauma. They have lost power and we need to empower them. In her book *The Hero Within*, Carol Pearson says: "The antidote to violence is not just self-control but self-knowledge and skills of self-expression and assertion."[81] In this book, I try to equip you with enough skills for self-expression and assertion, so that you can influence the behaviors of those who affect your emotional state.

PRACTICE:

Make the commitment to express your emotional hurts in a more constructive way. Learn to speak your feelings. I have noticed in my clinic that men find it easier to share "I felt disappointed." It is not exposing too much vulnerability. Maybe start with expressing this feeling of disappointment more often.

Empathize with your wife

Do you remember the last time someone said to you something like "I see how worried you are about that," or "I hear your disappointment"? How did it feel? These statements of validation often leave the other person feeling seen and understood. They are reassuring and calming. Your wife craves them. Being mindful of her needs and feelings reaches far into her heart.

Some men react with confusion upon hearing a request for empathy from their wives, responding with statements like "I am not good at that." Well, let me simplify it for you. You just need to structure your sentence so that you start with one of these statements: "I see..." or "I hear..." Make a brief statement to show her that you know how she feels. For example: "I see how it upsets you," "I hear your hurt," or "I hear your worries about it." It may sound like a little thing to say, but it will likely mean the world to your wife. You will connect with her pain rather than rush to fix it. This is strength and it is non-reactive. It's simple but not always easy to do.

Why?

Because your reactivity often gets in the way. As a Magician, you are mindful that these feelings are happening in her body, not yours. Observe it happening 'there,' not 'here.'

It is only when you realize your wife's dramas and pains that you are ready to provide the space she needs from you. This is one of the ways to "Hold her." Remember this extract from the opening quote in Chapter Three: "Hold her every time she needs to be held and you will always be her best lover ever."

To hold your wife when she is in pain, you will need to focus your attention on what she wants and needs. You will need to really see her to sense her vulnerabilities. She **particularly** needs your support when she is reactive, emotional, and stressed. Sure, her reactivity may trigger you, but this is the ultimate test for a Magician. Can you remain stoic and respond with empathy? Can you respond from a place of mindfulness and observation? Can you hold yourself first?

Very soon you will notice the reward for your empathy. Countless times I have heard women saying to their men with tears in their eyes: "This is all I have been asking for." Your wife will interpret genuine empathy as a sign of your care and love. And when your wife feels your care, her mood will be more positive. You will likely experience less resistance, fewer complaints, and more collaboration and support from her. This is how your empathy pays off.

PRACTICE:

Train yourself to respond with the formula "I see..." and "I hear..." to catch those moments when your wife is upset. If it feels awkward at the start, put a bit of humor around it. Tell her how you are training yourself to be the best husband and smile. She will laugh with you.

Coach her to start softly

In the King chapter, you learned about Gottman's core message to men: be open to accept influence from women. Now is the time to tell you his core message to women: Turn to him softly.

Since this book is aimed at what **you** can do to make a difference, in this case you will need a tool to coach your wife to start interactions softly. This is crucial for your relationship—make sure your interactions start with a gentle tone. You hate conflict, and this is how you will significantly reduce the chance of escalation.

Women initiate most marital interactions, so they are the ones who usually set the tone. This tone is like the starting point for a train—choose the track and you know where it ends. If your wife turns to you harshly, it may trigger your defensiveness. Her complaints and criticism are likely to hurt you. They can 'ring the alarm bell' of disapproval and potential rejection. They can trigger shame. "It feels like low-grade punches to my brain," is how one of my clients described it to me.

When your shame is triggered, it often leads to your unhelpful reactions of anger and withdrawal, which are likely to be met with more demands and criticism. To prevent this cycle, you must ensure she starts softly. This is one of your core missions because starting softly means less reactivity (shame, defensiveness) from you and more connection for you both.

Start by raising awareness. Tell her about the importance of starting softly. You may also use terms like "slowly," "gently," or "kindly"—whatever works for you both. Ask her to show consideration towards you. Explain the positive consequences for her—how it will get your attention to listen to what she wants, and help you remain engaged and be more willing to respond.

The next time your wife starts harshly (e.g., blaming, condemning, yelling, or criticizing), note mindfully the discomfort in your body. Instead of turning away or against her (a reactive option), turn towards her. This is by the principle of the Lover—always aim for engagement. Make her aware of how she affects you. For example:

- "It is hard to listen when you talk to me like that. Start with a nicer tone."
- "Can you talk to me more gently?"
- "Please try a positive start."
- "I don't like this tone. Try again please."
- "This is off-putting, you will have to talk differently if you want me to listen."

Then encourage her to simply state what she expects or wants. "So what do you want me to do?" or "How can I help?"

She will likely respond using negative terms like "Stop..." and "Don't..." Your job here is to get to the actionable request. In a highly reactive state, your wife may struggle to answer you. Help her define with clarity what she actually wants. Speaking what one wants is a sign of agency, a sign of power.

If she ignores your requests to change her tone and language, tell her **quietly** "You're losing me." If this hint is ignored, you must immediately and quietly take a break from the conversation. Tell her that you will continue to listen in a moment once you have both cooled down.

But if she can respond to your request, it's your turn to show your generosity. Find out what she wants and act on that as soon as possible! Rewarding good behavior works on us all, at all ages.

Remember that as creatures of habit, we don't change overnight. It may take many reminders before your wife internalizes your 'gentle tone' requests. She will keep hearing statements like "Gently please!" or "Slow down!" from you. One of my clients discovered that it was more helpful to use body language instead. He would gesture to calm down by using his hand and she got it. You will need to figure out what would work in your relationship

PRACTICE:

Set a relationship goal to make sure all your interactions with your wife start with a gentle tone and discuss this goal with her. Use the train on tracks metaphor and explain that you don't want to disengage.

Raise her awareness of how she turns to you affects how you respond.

Prime for positivity

Anxiety can make your wife—or any person—prone to negativity. Negativity includes assuming the worst, self-doubt, ruminating, complaining, mistrusting, blaming, being critical, and more. Don't fault the person, but the anxiety. This is how anxiety works. It makes you reactive and unsettled. Husbands are often exposed to a high level of negativity from their wives. Instead of reacting to the situation and escalating it, you can now use a different strategy.

In your capacity as a Magician, you can transform a negative chain of your wife's thoughts by gently directing her attention towards a more positive place. Directing a person's attention is a basic skill of a Magician. Use it to lead the conversation towards a positive tone with positive content and a positive outcome. The process is known as priming. You use stimuli to draw and direct attention. In conversations, words can be highly impactful. Certain words have a positive meaning and good energy associated with them. Use them intentionally to instantly transform the content and color of your conversations. For example:

- "Let's calm down" instead of "Don't stress."
- "Can you say something you appreciate?" instead of "Stop criticizing."
- "Go gently please" instead of "Don't be angry."
- "I have faith in you" instead of "You won't fail."
- "Use your kindness" instead of "Don't be so horrible."
- "We are resilient and we will manage" instead of "There's nothing to worry about."
- "I know how strong you are" instead of "Don't play the victim."

Apart from gaining a sense of community, many women are attracted to spiritual teaching for this reason—it provides solace to the soul through reflecting on positive ideas such as hope, connectedness (oneness), gratitude, faith, peace, and more. If you can inspire your wife with positivity (green filter), she will be immensely grateful. Consider learning the language of positivity together. As you both spend more time in the green filter, everyone wins.

PRACTICE:

Researchers in the field of positive psychology identify the following 24 character strengths which are valued in all cultures. Select the top 3 strengths for both you and your wife and ask her to do the same. Then discuss why you selected those strengths and how you fulfill them in your family.

1	creativity	13	kindness
2	curiosity	14	social intelligence
3	critical thinking	15	teamwork
4	gratitude	16	fairness
5	hope/optimism	17	leadership
6	love of learning	18	forgiveness
7	perspective/wisdom	19	modesty/humility
8	bravery	20	prudence/caution
9	perseverance	21	self-regulation/self-discipline
10	honesty/integrity	22	appreciation of beauty
11	zest/enthusiasm		and excellence
12	capacity to love/	23	humor/playfulness
	nurture close relationships	24	spirituality/purpose

Deal effectively with victimhood

For most of the history of mankind, men have held power and women have been dependent on them. The traditional female way to balance this power has been by sticking to principles of justice, keeping moral standards high, holding men accountable, and shaming them. Values of justice, equality, and fairness are more associated with the feminine. It is no accident that goddesses held the justice portfolio in mythology.

Justice and fairness are crucial values for a healthy society. But justice without a reality check is like freedom without order. The 'victim mentality' is an example of where we need a reality check because the unique mind filter plays a key role in this mentality, rather than reality. If your wife's filter interprets family drama through the prism of perceived fairness and equality, then there is a risk of her feeling victimized and exploited by you. In the cultural bug climate, women are regularly exposed to the injustice and victimhood narrative that portrays men as perpetrators and women as victims.

If your partner is sensitive to matters of equality, she may judge some situations as being 'unfair.' A perception of a lack of fairness breeds resentment and it can be dangerous to your relationship. For example: "I am with the kids all day while you fulfill your needs" or "I do so much around the house and you do almost nothing."

Getting defensive and argumentative in this situation is a big mistake. You need to follow the Magician path instead. First, listen with empathy to understand what is going on and what the pain is about. In most cases, the perceived issue is not the real issue; that is, her frustration may stem from lack of connection, self-doubts, or something else. It is hard for you to tell. However, if you believe it is a matter of perception, approach the issue as a scientist—ask, explore, and experiment by testing the reality to find facts. After all, your wife might have a point!

Rather than arguing about what has happened, ask her what she would like you to do to rectify the imbalance. Try to get as specific answers as possible. Negotiate and agree on what is fair, then act on the agreement.

But hang on, this is not the end. With highly sensitive people, justice needs to be seen, not only done. Track your contribution so that you are both aware of how well you complete your part of the agreement.

"Tell me your request and I will make you a queen."

Daniel had had enough of his wife bringing up past events. She was relentless in referring to past injustices and how he had hurt her. With 3 kids at home under the age of 5, her past childhood traumas, and a poor relationship with her parents, Daniel realized there was no way to win by reacting to her reactivity. He had to break out of this cycle.

Together Daniel and I designed this message to say to her: "I understand you are really hurt about the past, but I cannot do much about it. I really want to support you. I will not respond again to any mention of the past, but if you tell me your request, I promise to make you a queen."

She was teary and thanked him after he said it. The mood immediately changed in the household. She started to articulate her requests more and Daniel offered his support.

PRACTICE:

Think of an area in your marriage where your wife often brings up the fairness issue. Address it effectively with the reality check experiment and reach an agreement. Check with your wife from time to time about how satisfied she feels about what you do. If she is unhappy, treat it as feedback that something needs to be rectified.

Influence with written messages

You have probably noticed how communicating and talking are so important to your wife. This is how she connects to gain security. It is also how she expresses her verbal abilities, which are equivalent to you expressing your physical abilities. Spoken language means communication, which means connection, which means security. Verbal expression for females is more impactful and meaningful than it is for males. Males are more oriented towards action. This is one reason why counseling is far more appealing to women.

The tool I mentioned earlier—priming for positivity—is a way we can use the unique influence of verbal expression on the female mind. Some con men exploit that influence by manipulating women. Cult leaders do the same with their followers. Some men try to seduce women with smooth talk. The battered woman often says with confusion, "But he said he loves me." Sadly, hearing the words "I love you" can temporarily fix the pain of abuse.

It is worth mentioning here that we have another double standard in the use of language: your wife's negative words towards you carry a different weight if you say them to her. She will be more sensitive. This means that you should never match any of her negative language. In the next chapter on the Warrior, I share some ideas on how to address any hurtful language from your wife.

So, if the spoken language carries such power, what happens if we put messages in writing? Its power multiplies! Today, we constantly send text messages to our partners. These text messages carry the potential to both destroy and build.

Take advantage of the positive power of the writing tool. Write your positive messages to your partner via email or text. This tool is so powerful for several reasons.

1. You design your message with care and consideration. It is not impulsive, but thoughtful.

2. Written messages carry the additional value of intention and thoughtfulness.

3. It can be read and re-read.

4. There is less room for the 'filter' and wild interpretations if it is written.

5. The message can be read by others to get another perspective and a reality check.

6. A written message is 'evidence.' It is not 'hearsay.'

7. A written message is a document you can refer back to in the future.

Remember the slowness tool that I mentioned earlier in the chapter. The wise mind is not reactive and quick, but slow and considerate. Yes, written messages take more effort, but they can radically change relationships. I have seen it happen many times.

PRACTICE:

Develop the habit of texting positive messages to your wife. Consider writing a letter to express concerns and discuss hopes and expectations for a better future. It takes some effort, but gives you a great return on investment. Let the spiral of positivity take your relationship upward.

Takeaway messages to activate your Magician

Your purpose as a Magician is to transform reactivity into considered and workable solutions. Reactivity in family life stems from the attachment brain. It makes us vulnerable to fears of rejection, separation, and abandonment. Reactivity escalates conflict and creates negativity. It damages your relationship.

Use your capacity for being mindful and reflective to transform reactivity. Being mindful means observing and examining like a scientist before reacting. Your mindfulness creates a buffer against reactivity. When you do, you will give your family the gift of your clear and wise mind.

Your action plan

- Strengthen your capacity for being mindful because it will help you to self-regulate.
- Approach issues as a scientist and focus on what works.
- Practice noticing, naming, accepting, and responding slowly.
- Cultivate awareness of how shame affects you and learn to cope with it effectively.
- Transform your emotional flooding by using the power of words.
- Respond with empathy towards your wife's pains. Do not take them personally, and do not rush to fix them.
- Coach your wife to turn to you softly to guarantee that a constructive interaction ensues.
- Prime your conversation for a positive course by using words that evoke pleasant feelings.
- Apply reality check principles if you need to deal with the victimhood mentality.
- Write your important messages to make them more noticeable and impactful. Carefully select words that evoke 'yes.'

7

ACTIVATE YOUR WARRIOR TO
COMMAND RESPECT

"The Warrior is the basic building block of masculine psychology, almost certainly rooted in our genes... A Warrior knows what he wants, and he knows how to get it. A sense of danger energizes the man to take decisive action. This means that he engages life. He never withdraws from it... His actions become second nature."

— Robert Moore and Douglas Gillette, King, Warrior, Magician, Lover

Here is a brief reminder of the Warrior identity card that I described in more detail in Chapter Three.

My identity	I am a doer, a fighter, a protector, and a provider.
My purpose	To protect and provide for my family, accomplish goals, and succeed on missions.
How I work	I act, I take on challenges, I confront issues, I assert boundaries.

Her voice:

"I can tolerate many of your annoying behaviors, but seeing you weak is unsettling for me. I need you to stand strong; strong with your will, strong with your position, and strong with your words. I need you to be a man. Yes, even if I am a passionate feminist! Living in a female body, I am vulnerable. Recall how protective you are with our daughter. You understand how the world can be unsafe for women at any time and in any place. I need to know that you are strong and can stand up for me, for us.

*But can you stand up **for** me if you can't stand up **to** me?!*

If you avoid conflicts because you are afraid; if you are too dependent on me; if you lose it with emotional outbursts; if you don't know what you want in your life; if you are a pushover; all of these things make me feel like I am living with a boy, not a man. You are guaranteed to lose my respect. Pleasing me to keep the peace will only achieve the opposite result. I may please people in order to be liked, but it often comes at a great cost. I don't want you to do the same. You win my respect when I appreciate how you assert your boundaries, and how you look after yourself, your interests, your career, and us as a family. Please be strong for us so we can feel safe."

The Warrior is the most obvious masculine role in a relationship. Evolution has shaped the kind of traits in men that are most needed for the mission of raising a family—protecting and providing. Evolutionary psychology research confirms that these traits are what women desire in a potential partner.[82] Women in all cultures tend to seek the same kind of Warrior qualities in a man: strength, confidence, status, assertiveness, and ambition. These traits increase the chance of him protecting her and providing the resources she needs when she raises babies.

And what about successful women in modern rich nations? They expect the same traits. The forces of evolution speak louder than the forces of culture when it comes to the projects of mating and raising a family. Women like men to capitalize on their masculine strengths associated with the Warrior. Hence, her expectations from you in your role as a Warrior will be the most urgent and crucial for her. In the hierarchy of her needs, your Warrior capacities to protect and provide come at the top because they complement her vulnerabilities right where she needs you the most as a man—for the safety and security of herself and her children.

However, as much as women expect these qualities from men, the messages men get in our culture are conflicting and confusing. These messages make the Warrior role the most controversial and troubling for men. Warrior qualities are highest on the list of female expectations, but it's also the most condemned role. Yes, she would like you to celebrate your testosterone by having high energy and being dynamic, goal-oriented, and powerful. But at the same time, your masculinity is under attack for other qualities that go hand in hand with the mindset of a Warrior, such as competitiveness, dominance, and the suppression of emotions.

The humiliating concept of "toxic masculinity" refers to our Warrior qualities. The Warrior captures the essence of masculinity and an attack on masculinity is an attack on the Warrior. It is therefore an attack on the very important traits that women tend to want to find in men. This is why men and women should fight together against the emasculating nature of the cultural bug.

Even if she is a feminist, your wife will be the least forgiving if you underperform in your Warrior role. Being not good enough as a Warrior may breed her contempt, and contempt is the strongest predictor of divorce. Due to her vulnerabilities and security needs, she can't tolerate seeing you 'unmanly' and weak—that is, being immature, lazy, needy, impulsive, moody, non-dependable, a push-over, and lacking perseverance. She needs to respect you as the man in her life. In his book *The Way of Men*, Jack Donovan makes the point that commanding respect is the clearest difference between being a "good man" and "being good at being a man."[83] Our *Good Husband* project is about being good at being a man.

Warriors are protectors of their family and their interests. They keep their wives safe by asserting boundaries and deflecting threats. Today these threats are mostly social and emotional, such as conflicts with in-laws or members of the community. Women in our safe and prosperous democracies rarely need their men to risk their life to protect them, but occasionally we get a reminder of the threats that require men to take on this traditional physical role as Warriors and protectors.

For example, in the recent war in Ukraine, most women and children escaped the country while most men stayed behind to fight. A TV news report I watched showed two boys aged seven and nine asked what their father told them before saying goodbye. The answer was, " We are men and we should protect Mum." Another woman explained why her husband stayed behind: "He must fight with the other men, otherwise he will lose self-respect." When the world faces dangerous leaders, the idea of turning men away from their 'traditional masculinity' proves to be really bad. The Warrior is a force for good and his masculinity should be honored and celebrated.

If the traditional role of the Warrior is to defend his family and country against external threats, the Warrior in a modern family needs to protect more against internal threats. One source of these internal threats is the immaturity and confusion of many men about their masculine role and identity. The other source of internal threats is angry partners who treat their husbands with disrespect, and at times, even abuse.

These two types of threats are interrelated and linked to the cultural change in the way partners negotiate power and decision-making in modern family life. Failing to deal effectively with these internal threats results in a tragic loss of respect that affects everyone in the family. The focus of the modern Warrior husband should be on commanding respect within his own family.

The Warrior in you serves your King—the part of you that represents your values, vision, honor, family, and nation. As a King, you should be clear about what life wants from you, your purpose, and what is important for you, so that your Warrior can get into action. A warrior is willing to sacrifice and endure pain to achieve his life's purpose.

Commanding respect

You command respect in two ways: directly and indirectly. The direct way is the assertive way, in which you ask people to treat you respectfully if they don't already. The indirect way is by inspiring others to see you as an honorable man worthy of their respect. The word 'respect' is derived from the Latin *respicere*, which means "to look again." When we respect, we pay attention. We see people in their own right, rather than solely through the filter of our own needs and interests. The opposite is to ignore, to disregard, to exploit, to hurt and to see a person as a means to an end. For example, if you see your wife as a means to getting sex, then you don't respect her. If she sees you as a means of getting financial security, then she doesn't respect you.

To command respect means you expect to be seen and considered. You do that through your actions and integrity. You prove that you are worthy of respect. Creating order with your King energy is where you start to win respect, but at times that is not enough. These are the times when your King needs your Warrior to fight for your realm, your family, and your core values. You need your Warrior when your woman treats you unkindly, or when someone hurts her or your kids.

Why should you command respect?

As strange as it may sound, you should command respect for your family's benefit, not just for yourself. When your children and wife respect you, it means that they trust you and value your role in the family. They need these things as much as you do.

As the Warrior, you protect the role of your King to create order. Your Warrior energy serves your King. The respect I am talking about is not to your self-image or ego, but rather to your family role and responsibilities. Your voice matters; your words are important. You expect everyone to show respect towards the authority in your family, which of course includes respect towards both of you—the King and the Queen of the house. Respect is powerful when you tell your kids off for disrespecting their mother. It is always a winner.

Without respect, your wife will perceive you as weak. She will take you for granted, she will dismiss your input, she will resent you, she will lose interest in sex with you and, ultimately, she may lose interest in you as a partner.

In addition, when you command respect, you also give respect. It goes both ways. The immature husband wants to be the center of his wife's attention, so he fails to show consideration for her needs. She doesn't feel that he 'sees' her. No wonder she loses respect for him.

When you command respect, you also help your wife with her boundaries. Women tend to do a good job at being liked but far worse at being respected. Commanding respect is the Warrior quality we should hope to teach our daughters—aspire to be respected, not just liked.

Protect your own boundaries from confusion and self-doubt. Your wife needs you to hold your fortress strong in terms of its boundaries. When you stand up **to** her, it reassures her that you can stand up **for** her. Just like any other human being, you deserve to be respected. Unconditionally. And this is also a good message to teach and model to your children.

Finally, there is one more good reason that men should command respect in their families: to stop the negative spiral of today's boys becoming tomorrow's non-assertive men. Boys are often raised by protective mothers whose voices are getting louder by the day to demand more "safety," to stop "microaggressions," and more. The ramifications of this phenomenon are described in the book *The Coddling of the American Mind: How Good Intentions and Bad Ideas Are Setting Up a Generation for Failure.*[84] As the title implies, children who grow up in an over-protective environment fail to develop the tough and resilient mindset needed to meet life's challenges.

That's how the spiral works. Boys are raised in 'liberal' homes, by 'liberated' women, free from the 'patriarchal hierarchy.' This environment strengthens the female voice while weakening the male voice. It may tilt the balance towards more protectiveness and less challenge. One resulting side- effect is children who are spoiled, indulged, and over-protected. Now that these boys have become husbands, it haunts them. They present as immature men who expect their partners to replace their mothers. Women often condemn them as "narcissists." However, these men need to cope with a gap in their character building. They now need to work harder and make conscious efforts to develop the Warrior mindset—discipline, resilience, and responsibility. As a father, you can make sure things turn out differently for your boys. I elaborate on that further in Chapter Nine.

How men lose respect

The cultural bug may have made things a bit harder for men, but our working assumption has not changed—any loss of respect for you is ultimately based on what you do or don't do. You need to act and lead your life as an agent of change, not in reaction to others. A sense of agency is at the core of the Warrior identity.

There are several ways in which men lose respect.

1. **Failing to provide**

   Your wife's most basic expectation of you is that you provide for your family when she is busy raising children. This is as primal as your expectation of her to take good care of your kids. Her hardwired desire is that you provide resources that give the family security. You will lose her respect if you don't fulfill this basic desire. She will be worried, and her family and friends may share their worries too.

Further, a man's identity is largely defined by his career and success. Your wife would like to see you happy, fulfilled, and proud of yourself even if she is a strong provider herself.

2. **Addictive behaviors**

    Any addiction will compromise you from being a leader in your life. Drugs, alcohol, and any other addiction will distract your attention, making you unreliable for your wife. This will be extremely disturbing for her. You will have betrayed the King in you (by not creating order and living according to your values). Your wife may feel disdain towards you.

3. **Emotional immaturity**

    Many men have grown up in homes with a passive or absent father. Such a family system often creates mutual dependency between a mother and her child, and the child becomes the center of her attention. When the boy grows up, he brings these expectations to his wife. She resents it. She may condemn him as a "narcissist" for his high demands on her.

4. **Conflict avoidance**

    This behavior is typical of "nice guys" who try to please their partners to avoid conflicts and confrontation. The passive, non-confrontational approach makes their wives look down on them. These men are not asserting their boundaries, and their wives worry that their men won't stand up for them in their times of need. "Man up," these women may say to their husbands in frustration.

5. **Unkind treatment**

    Women today will show little tolerance for inconsiderate, unkind, or aggressive behaviors. They—very rightly—

expect respect. However, if a man treats his wife unkindly, he reveals that he doesn't respect himself. After all, his wife is part of his life; if he doesn't respect her, he doesn't respect himself.

6. Fear of divorce

Statistically, the possibility of divorce is a real threat. Men seem to dread it, and women tend to use the threat of divorce far more often. Fear weakens the man, and a woman doesn't like her man to be afraid of her.

Loss of respect is a widespread and highly disturbing experience that men can feel in marriage. Too often I hear stories of aggression by wives towards their husbands, and even abuse. What I have been witnessing in my clinic is a well-documented social trend, but we don't hear much about it. Men's pain in relationships hardly makes its way to the news, not to mention their pain from losing their families. A US survey found that 1 in 4 men suffered physical violence from their partners, while for women the rate was 1 in 3.[85] As mentioned earlier, a female former police officer in Australia stated in a YouTube interview that in her 13 years on the job more than half of the violent incidents were instigated by women.[86]

There are also forms of psychological abuse by partners— insulting, belittling, shaming, yelling, verbally abusing, controlling contact with family or friends, and turning the children against the other partner or threatening to take them away. In Australia, partner psychological abuse is about the same for both sexes.[87]

The way society views domestic violence by female partners creates an immense bias in reporting the phenomenon, in legislation, and ultimately, in governmental policies. Men suffer greatly from this bias but often contribute to it by not telling their stories. Instead, they cover and suppress their emotional hurt. It is hard to tell the facts from the narrative. To find the truth on the extent of males being the victims of female partner violence, we need a way to only measure behavior and bypass the filters that create the reporting bias, such as perception, meaning, intention, and impact. We need to count each act of aggression, regardless of the context or consequence; a female slap should be counted just the same as a male slap.

This is what sociology professor Murray Straus looked at with his "Conflict Tactics Scales" tool.[88] The tool exposed a different reality to the common narrative. In their tactics to resolve conflicts, Straus found that men and women are fairly equal in their use of aggression. The most significant difference is that men strike harder with more damaging consequences. Straus is an expert in the field of domestic violence, but immediately felt the impact of the cultural bug. In response to suggesting an equivalence between the male and female tendency toward family aggression, he was 'excommunicated' by feminists overnight.

A similar fate happened to Erin Pizzey, a feminist hero who founded Britain's first women's refuge in 1971. Years later she published a book about violent women and argued that men and women could be equally cruel.[89] She became an advocate for the men's rights movement and was removed from the history of the feminist movement.

Counselor and relationship coach Ann Silvers challenged the silence surrounding males being abused by female partners in her book *Abuse OF Men By Women*. She describes how various ways of emotional and physical abuse (such as controlling, manipulating, threatening, and bullying) hurt men badly, as the subtitle of her book suggests: *It happens, it hurts, and it's time to get real about it.*[90] More data on the prevalence of intimate partner violence against men can be found in Philip Cook's book *Abused Men: The Hidden Side of Domestic Violence.*[91] Bettina Arndt is a well-known advocate for men. In both her book *#MenToo*[92] and YouTube channel,[93] Arndt exposes the truth about aggression against men, as well as the anti-male bias in court, in policies, and in media coverage.

When it comes to domestic violence, many experts like these agree that the approach towards it is tainted by the cultural bug—ideology before truth, victimhood and blame before responsibility and empowerment. The dominant victimhood narrative is that men are the perpetrators and women the victims. The voice of men who suffer humiliation, abuse, and loss of contact with their kids is hardly heard. Men themselves rarely dare to confront this narrative because it may result in conflicts with their partners. It is safer to belong to the 'righteous' group and appear as white knights. By the time they become the next victims, they are often too angry to effectively advocate for their fellow men.

That said, we do not want to treat men as victims. To pity them with the victimhood narrative is to look down on them and further reduce their respect. Men need tools and guidance to reclaim their power and command respect. This is what the sense of agency means. I have always been passionate about empowering women when they suffer from male aggression, and I apply the same passion to empowering men. Enough with the double standards.

The impact on husbands

When a man is shamed, blamed, or attacked by his wife, he feels profoundly vulnerable. After all, this is the very person he wishes to care for and protect. She is the object of his love. In the old days, some men might have used their physical strength to deter their wives from such attacks, but those old methods of control and intimidation are rightly seen both morally and legally as being unacceptable today.

However, without alternative ways to negotiate their power, many men are at a loss. They often lack the verbal skills to describe how they feel. They grieve privately and withdraw into themselves with a deep sense of failure and shame. Shame makes them hide and suppress, rather than reach out for support and share their pain. This is a silent killer that hardly anyone talks about. And even if men do share their stories, they barely get any support because of the bias against them. Sadly, men are left very alone in how they manage their hurt from psychologically aggressive wives. Their hurts are not heard, and therefore not validated. Psychological aggression from wives doesn't leave bruises on the body but scars the husbands' souls. The emotional toll of powerlessness and helplessness is immense.

Let's reflect on how these feelings affect men. Powerlessness may breed male rage, and rage leads to acts of aggression and violence. A society contaminated by the cultural bug can push a man to believe that his manifested anger is the issue rather than his deep feelings of hurt, powerlessness, and shame. Such men are typically referred to "anger management" programs. Some of these programs teach superficial self-control techniques that are fruitless and only further humiliate men. In fact, what these men need are tools to help them express their powerlessness and vulnerabilities. They need to learn how to negotiate effectively so they are heard and their needs are met. They need to reclaim their power just like women learn to do.

The paradox is that in all practicality, those violent and scary men are very weak. They fail miserably to manage the process of conflict—to express what they feel and need. They fail to influence their partner. Aggression toward their wives is surely not a sign of a Warrior energy, but weakness. Those men who are in jail for assaulting their wives do not prove 'patriarchal tyranny,' but how miserable and pathetic men can become when they lack skills to influence their partners and to settle differences with effective communication tools. They have failed the basic entry test to the Warrior club—honor and self-control. Even the other criminals in jail look at them with disdain.

Helplessness may breed depression in these men. Depression often causes further avoidance and self-withdrawal, often accompanied by some form of substance abuse. Avoidance is a killer of connection and men who avoid their wives make them even more frustrated and angry. As the cycle escalates, so does the sense of hopelessness and despair. Something goes terribly wrong for these men, but they often remain invisible to their community.

It is hard for an abused man to believe anyone will listen to him with understanding and empathy. The perception abounds that his wife is more vulnerable, more sensitive, more moral, more fair, and therefore must be right. Emotionally abused men are left helpless. In their despair, a few of these men might cowardly turn to extreme options. Out of rage they may try to harm their wives, and out of depression they may try to harm themselves. Many cases of male suicide resulting from a breakup never come to our awareness because it is hard to prove the cause of suicide.

Men need to find their own way to command respect as a matter of urgency. No one is going to do that for them. Men should treat aggression towards them just as they would have treated aggression toward women—with zero tolerance. You must reclaim your power so you do not end up feeling powerless and helpless. Those feelings are toxic. Reclaim your power for the benefit of everyone in your family—your wife, your kids, and yourself.

The meaning of aggression in the family

Aggression in the family is a sign of powerlessness. Parents hit children and partners hurt each other because they fail to deal effectively with loss of power. They use ineffective tools to influence another person to respond to their needs. Powerlessness breeds anxiety, inadequacy, failure, shame, and helplessness. It has a long-term negative impact on both mental and physical health. When these feelings build up, rage and explosions may follow.

I express my belief throughout this book that when partners are empowered with a good understanding of their issues and effective tools to address them, they become a better version of themselves. So keep in mind that when you or your partner resort to aggressive methods, it doesn't mean you are being bad. It means you are being very vulnerable.

If your wife is aggressive, regard it as a strong sign of her feelings of powerlessness and weakness. Her aggression must be stopped at once so that you can offer her the support she needs.

In my work with aggressive husbands, I have found that being empathetic helps them to learn new ways to express their vulnerabilities and needs. It works the same for an aggressive wife who needs to recognize the pain underlying her rage.

Barriers to commanding respect

The possibility of some men confronting their wives for their aggression can be daunting for them. Fear stops them from taking a clear stand. The fear of escalating the conflict that they dread so badly. Fear of their wives' disapproval, rejection, and ultimately the fear of losing them. These fears can be paralyzing. Men need their wives (and vice versa), because this is how love works.

Recall your attachment brain. When we are attached to someone, we run on the same mechanism we see in young children—we seek closeness to survive. On a deep, subconscious level we treat our partners as caretakers. We rely on them to be there for us in times of need. This is why ordinary conflicts may provoke extreme reactivity in us. The threat of losing connection is very frightening indeed.

Losing your wife might be scary if you rely on her for all your emotional and social needs. There is so much at stake for you. Unfortunately, this is the case for too many men. It is like investing all your socioemotional assets in just one share on the stock market. It's a terrible mistake.

Tragically, men's fears only make matters worse. Fear makes you avoid, freeze, or attack. Men who fear conflict want to be liked and approved rather than respected. Women do not seem to appreciate that. This is because avoiding conflicts and confrontation means avoiding their resolution. The avoidance frustrates her. She regards it as a sign of weakness. Seeing you as weak might make her feel disdain and contempt towards you. She may judge and shame you.

Your partner expects you to "hold her while she is mad" (as outlined in Chapter Three). Holding is used here as a metaphor for holding the situation rather than physically holding her. It means to stay present, close, and centered. A fearful man is a turn-off for her as he isn't capable of addressing her security needs. Think of the 'nice guy' who is trying to appease and avoid conflict only to face more of his partner's frustration and rage. A man needs Warrior qualities to deal with his fears, so let's explore them now.

PRACTICE:

Have a discussion with your wife about respect. Here are some ideas for leading questions.

- Who is a person in your life that you respect?
- Why?
- When do I win your respect and when do I lose it?

The Warrior way

Courage is the defining characteristic of Warriors. Being courageous is not a spontaneous act. It is a value, and may I add, it's my favorite value. As a child growing up in Israel, I felt deeply inspired by stories of heroic acts that took place during the Holocaust and the wars of Israel. Threats—real or imagined—cause fear. Fear stops and paralyzes us. It makes us avoid instead of act. We can face our fears with courage. They are 'dragons' that we slay to complete our mission. Let's look at how Warriors manifest courage.

Action

Action is the hallmark of the Warrior. To achieve his goal, he must act. The mission is accomplished only after some effort and a few battles. The myth of the Warrior is that he must slay some dragons on his way to the castle at the top of the hill. Metaphorically, these dragons represent external obstacles as much as those within him.

In the marriage context, these dragons are the fears that stop you from acting in the best interests of yourself and your family. Avoidance and withdrawal are the antithesis of the Warrior's energy. The Warrior shows up in the family by engaging, confronting, and resolving issues. Avoidance means fear, but Warriors are always in a mode of moving forward towards achieving their goals. If you want to cultivate the energy of the Warrior, then strong physical activity or participating in competitive sport will be your best bet.

Overcoming challenges

Warriors love challenges! In fact, they go after them. "Bring them on," they shout before the match. Overcoming challenges means overcoming resistance and obstacles, solving problems, and enduring some pain. They approach problems with enthusiasm because they are opportunities to prove themselves and practice their skills. Warriors grow with each challenge they tackle. Overcoming challenges stretches and builds their character as doers and achievers. It strengthens Warrior qualities such as resilience, perseverance, steadfastness, and resourcefulness.

During dating, many females are turned on by the male's drive to 'conquer' their hearts. His attempts to overcome her resistance prove his determination and focus. These are promising traits for a successful provider. She intuitively knows his Warrior capacities by the way he meets challenges and resistance.

Authenticity

Social fears such as rejection and shame make people pretend and mask their truth. They may sacrifice their genuine interests in their attempt to be liked and approved. But Warriors stand up for what they believe and don't shrink from confrontations or peer pressure. They speak their mind. They understand that expressing themselves authentically does not compromise their other important values such as kindness. Authenticity is about being loyal to your values as much as to your interests, needs, and wants. This is how self-respect feels.

A sense of agency

Warriors are reliable soldiers in the service of the King. They are passionate about their freedom to act. They cannot be puppets for anyone but the King's values (the 'right' way). Their freedom is linked directly to their sense of self-respect.

A sense of agency implies that you are in charge of your own life. You bear responsibility, not guilt, for whatever happens to you, even when something is clearly not your fault. To command respect, Warriors must establish their self-identity as the ultimate agent for anything that happens in their lives. It is a position of power, not a recipe for guilt or blame.

Self-discipline

Mastery over the mind and emotions is crucial for a Warrior's success. The demanding and high- risk tasks that he often engages in require him to be clear and focused. Warriors cannot afford confusion, hesitation, distraction, or too much thinking. Decisive action can save lives. To guarantee precision and success in their tasks, Warriors develop self-discipline and self-control.

Many people learn martial arts for this very purpose—to build emotional stability and self-regulation through training in the art of fighting.

Operating with a code of honor

Warriors operate with a code of honor. They are committed to certain honorable behaviors such as keeping their word, being loyal to friends during combat, and persisting on a mission. Their honor is linked to their tasks and responsibility. As they consolidate their skills and reputation, they strengthen their sense of honor and self-respect. What they offer has great value and they expect this value to be recognized. You will recognize an honorable Warrior by the respect he pays to his fellow men. Immature men tend to be intimidated by other men, while the injured ones are too keen to attack other men (like injured dogs do).

Resilience

Warriors may occasionally fail or lose, but their fighting spirit means that they keep trying. They don't give up. In the context of marriage, resilience means bouncing back after a bad vibe or conflict. In her book *Mindset: The New Psychology of Success*, researcher Carol Dweck explains that it is not talent but hard work and perseverance that ultimately separates highly successful people from others. They share a healthy mindset of treating mistakes and failures as opportunities for learning.[94] Failures tell you nothing about who you are, but a lot about the lessons you are supposed to learn. If you resist these lessons, explore what stops you from listening to what life is trying to teach you.

Victimhood is taboo, but not vulnerability

The Warrior is too busy getting to the goal or the solution. Victimhood is a distraction. Therefore, he doesn't want to spend energy on arguing, complaining, or protesting. Driven by his future goals, the Warrior will focus on "**what**" rather than "**why**" questions. He may ask himself, "What should I do here?" or ask others "What do you want?". Such 'what' questions connect you with your agent within and inspire action.

Tread lightly with the 'why' questions because they lead to seeking answers that are in the past. In the context of a relationship, "why" questions often lead to the blame game and victimhood. Victimhood is good for winning sympathy and support, and we may need it occasionally. But keep it as the exception, since victimhood and entitlement run opposite to the Warrior's energy.

It is a big mistake to place your power in the hands of others. For example, my second child is adopted and his Ethiopian background means he has nearly always been the only black person in our neighborhood. As a child, this fact could have exposed him to racist comments. Yet he has hardly ever complained about any racism towards him. Not only because he is a very likable person, but because victimhood has never been an option in his mind. You either confront the person or move away.

On the other hand, Warriors do acknowledge vulnerability. They don't regard vulnerability as a weakness, but as a part of being human. Acknowledging their pains and fears sets them up to get the support they need. Being aware of their limitations and lack of knowledge only opens them up to learning new skills and tools. The Warrior's agenda is to hone his capacities to perform best on his missions.

Anger serves the Warrior

Anger for a Warrior is a healthy emotion that can serve to energize him into action. Anger is a sign that someone violates, threatens, or hurts us. It is a sign of injustice. It is a call for action. For example, a coach may secretly hope that the supporters of the opposing team verbally abuse his players. Why? Because this is guaranteed to fuel his players. So, regard anger as a gift from nature to help us defend ourselves against threats to our interests, body, family, and nation.

Anger has a bad reputation and we need to change that. When you fail to mobilize anger constructively, you end up either suppressing it, or expressing it in passive-aggressiveness or even explosive tempers. These are signs that your anger scares you! It paralyzes you, rather than mobilizes you. A healthier attitude would be to embrace and utilize it as a Warrior. The authentic expression of anger is assertiveness. This is when your courage, rather than fear, meet your anger.

One possible reason people fear anger is that they confuse it with aggression. Anger and aggression are two different things! We are against aggression, but not against anger. If you are treated unkindly by your partner, it will hurt you and may make you experience anger. Your anger is valid, but when expressing it, you need to make sure that your anger does not become her fear. A woman may easily get scared around men's anger because of its short distance from aggression. To command respect and set boundaries as a Warrior, you need to express your anger constructively. Read on to learn how you can.

THE WARRIOR IN ACTION

There are a variety of tools that you can use to activate your Warrior to command respect, including:

- fulfilling your mission as a provider,
- taking care of yourself,
- slaying the 'divorce dragon',
- slaying the 'shame dragon',
- protecting your realm,
- swiftly ending any aggressive episodes, and
- preparing for the battle over your children.

Let's look at each tool in more detail.

Fulfill your mission as a provider

Women today want to do just as well as men when it comes to careers and salaries, but one thing has not changed: Many women still judge and measure men by their earning capacity. Evolutionary psychologist David Buss says "a man's ability to provide a woman with the resources is central to his mate value, her selection of him as a partner, and the tactics men use to attract and retain women."[95] In one study of ten thousand people in 37 countries, women placed far greater value than men did on good financial prospects.

As the main caretaker of your young children, it makes sense why your wife expects you to take good care of your family's finances. That is her security. Her expectations are fair and reasonable from an evolutionary perspective. She gives birth and cares for the babies and you provide for them. If you do not do your part in this deal well enough, this might be a big concern for her. It may even create a trust crisis. Just imagine if you were unhappy with how she looks after your babies.

Your wife appreciates how success at work matters to your self-image and how **you** judge yourself. Our work has so much to do with our identity as men, and how worthy we feel about ourselves. We actualize ourselves through our work. Your wife would like to see you as a fulfilled Warrior who takes pride in what you do and your accomplishments. When your work is not fulfilling or unstable, the impact on everyone in your family is very hard.

For many women, your commitment to success at work equates with commitment to yourself and your family. If this area in your life is not on track or not yet settled, then you may lose your wife's respect. Give it your highest priority and don't bank on her feminism to give you any concessions here. When unemployed clients come to me for help, my standard response is that 'getting back on the horse' is far more urgent than treating psychological issues.

PRACTICE:

Make your family proud of what you do and your accomplishments. If you don't have a job, this should be your highest priority before focusing on any other idea in this book. Your career should receive its due regard as the foundation of your self-respect as a man.

Take care of yourself

A Warrior can only be as strong as his mental and physical strength allows. Taking care of yourself connects to the Warrior attribute of commanding respect. Looking after your mind and body is essential for success in your missions. Jordan Peterson put it this way: "*You are important to other people, as much as to yourself. You have some vital role to play in the unfolding destiny of the world. You are, therefore, morally obliged to take care of yourself.*"[96]

However, highly dedicated men to their missions often fail to live by this simple truth. They neglect their health and social life, relying too heavily on their wives for their well-being. As we learned earlier, placing so much in the hands of one person in your life may expose you to profound vulnerability if there is a crisis in the relationship. The threat of losing your wife may then be paralyzing.

Take care of your physical health, your hygiene, and your appearance. This may sound strange, but these self-care basics are not that obvious for many men. Recall that respect means to see and consider a person. These basic self-care steps are statements of self-respect. You matter to yourself first.

Take care of your mental health. If your mood or addiction affects your behavior, then your life is not in order. Instead of being an asset, you become a liability to your wife. You stop being reliable and you lose her respect. Countless times women have said to me that they feel as if they are dealing with another child in the family when describing their husbands. It's no surprise that these women are not up for sex with their partners. Who wants to go to bed with a kid?!

Take care of your social life and diversify your emotional investments beyond your wife. Women do this well with their social networks, and we should learn from them. Don't put all your eggs in that one basket that is your wife. Instead, learn from her and cultivate social networks and hobbies of your own. Strengthening your relationships with your male friends will benefit you in several ways:

- Their energy will boost your masculine energy because men tend to think and do things in manly ways, such as challenging and competing with each other.

- Your male friends are a resource for learning and expanding beyond your comfort zone.

- Your male friends may offer support during difficult times with your partner.

A man who connects with his mates and appreciates and supports them is a mature man who is comfortable in his self-identity. On the other hand, a man who avoids other men or is afraid of them has not reached maturity in his sense of manhood. View other men not only as your competitors, but also as your mirror and your coaches. We can learn so much from each other. Taking care of your health and emotional and social needs will guarantee that your Warrior is well equipped for your mission.

PRACTICE:

Find one or two things you can do to improve your self-care practice. Commit to doing them and ask your wife to hold you accountable.

Reflect on those male friends with whom you would like to cultivate your friendship, and reach out to them.

Consider a new hobby to expand your social network.

Slay the 'D' (divorce) dragon

For generations, marriage was something men and women committed to for life. Divorce was a remote option. Partners knew that even if they argued or fought, it would not end their relationship. It simply meant some unpleasant feelings during tense moments, and couples developed resilience around them. That level of commitment also meant security and the ability to tolerate some level of conflict.

However, we are now at a point where many partners approach marriage with heavy doubts about its long-term sustainability and viability. These new expectations are wreaking havoc on the mission of loving and committed relationships that create a secure environment. The sad paradox is that the easy-exit divorce option exacerbates partners' break-up anxiety. This anxiety only worsens the reactions to conflicts and pushes partners further to the edge of the abyss with each fight. Many partners have lost the capacity to argue like two loyal friends do—without the risk of dumping each other. Tragically, the fear of separation has now turned into a self-fulfilling prophecy. Instead of more freedom, the easy-exit option has created more fear.

Your wife will probably threaten you with divorce at some stage. This is what women tend to do these days when they feel stuck and powerless in their relationships. (By the way, men are not more righteous here. They don't usually threaten divorce, but they may seek a lover.)

Women's divorce threats often have a big impact. Men get scared. However, seeing their men react with fear is a turn-off for their wives. It only makes wives feel more contempt towards their men. By now you should realize that the enemy is the fear in your heart, not your wife's dramatic statement of despair. You do need to listen to her underlying pain and respond kindly, but it is essential to do so only after you crack down on any threatening language.

Threats of separation are a form of emotional abuse. Recall the mechanism of attachment and you'll realize that the threat of separation is like threatening a child with placement in a foster family if he behaves badly. This is a betrayal. It hurts because it goes straight to the core of your need for security. You suddenly feel exposed.

Being threatened is humiliating. In the Warrior's code of honor, this is unacceptable. This moment is a mega-test for your courage. Your response must be swift. Appeasing your wife will only feed the 'divorce dragon.' You have to slay it instead.

But let's look closely at this dragon first.

The little boy within you tells you that you cannot live without your wife—her presence is essential for your ability to cope with life's challenges. You have turned her into the linchpin that holds you together. Without her, you will crumble and feel lost and isolated. You suddenly find yourself on the edge of the abyss of endless darkness and uncertainty.

As you listen carefully to this little boy, you'll realize that he expects your wife to function as a mother figure, not as the woman in his life. The power you have placed in her hands is now exposing your dependency needs and your vulnerability. As if she is holding your balancing pole while you are walking a tightrope between two buildings. No wonder you are terrified. If your wife feels so much power, there is a risk not only that she may use it to exert pressure and manipulate you, but also to look at you with disdain. You will lose her respect!

This is a wake-up message. If you feel this way, it's time to activate your Warrior and grow into a mature man.

For a start, take a moment to reflect on the story of that little boy. Engage your Magician for the sake of self-examination and self-awareness. A marriage breakup is a scary and painful experience; there's no doubt about it. But can you see it as a setback you can overcome? A loss you will recover from? It is a test of your Warrior spirit—how resilient, assertive, proud, and independent you are. Recognizing your mental strength will guarantee your freedom to act in the service of your King for the sake of your core values and your self-respect. This is the time to tap into your courage.

You need courage to handle both the external threat and your vulnerability within. Your wife's threatening divorce tactic should be the last time you experience it. It's time to have a conversation in which you drive home a strong and clear message. It is not enough to just say "Don't threaten." The outcome of the conversation should be a commitment from both of you never to use the tactic of threatening because it is a severe blow to trust. It is a betrayal.

Consider a confrontational message like this:

"You are threatening and I don't want to ever hear any threats. That is emotional abuse. If you want to divorce, arrange a meeting with a lawyer and I will come. Until then, please use the normal ways to express your feelings, or suggest a third party that we can both consult."

In the ensuing conversation, make it clear that if your relationship ever ends in divorce, the kids will be with you at least 50% of the time. This will put to rest any delusion she might have about an easy outcome for her. The conversation should end with this request: "Can we agree that we never use threats like that on each other?"

When divorce is a serious option on the table, partners talk about it with deep grief, not as a threat. After all, even if you do choose to divorce, you should maintain respect for each other.

Now to the courage you will need for your vulnerability within. This is the courage you need to admit your mistakes and face your shame. As her husband, you hate seeing your wife in pain. You want to support her, but you may not know how. Your anger or avoidance are signs of your helplessness rather than your desire to punish or reject her. Sadly, most wives fail to recognize this truth, and most husbands fail to convey it properly. Dare to open your heart and admit that you really want to help, but you are not sure how. Talk to her openly about your struggle. Regard your wife as someone who wants to support you.

Hang on a moment. Does your wife really mean it if she threatens divorce? In most cases I have been privy to, wives didn't, at least initially. They are just expressing their powerlessness and fear. They feel disconnected, lonely, and unsupported. If anything, it is more the threat they feel about losing the love of their men. Your wife may suspect you have given up on her and your relationship. To find out the truth, she may test your motivation to fight for her.

Yet another reason altogether is that her pain has nothing to do with you, but is all about her self-loathing and self-doubts. The risk of such feelings is high if she has doubts about her motherhood and her relationship with the kids. At the end of the day, this is her vulnerability chucked over to your turf of vulnerability with the hope that you feel her pain and find the courage to help both of you. Keep this option in your heart.

But what if she insists on divorce?

Sadly, quite a few men fail to cope constructively with the pain of separation. For some of them, this leads to disaster. This is a moment to tap into your masculine strengths.

The *Good Husband* will stick to his values and mature masculinity, even when she wants to stop being married to you. Do so for your own sake and the sake of your children. This is your toughest test to see how you hold yourself 'together' during such a stressful time—continuing to maintain the 'throne' even when your Queen leaves is your entitlement. It is how you prove your worth and your power. But if the possibility of divorce undermines your emotional stability to the point of abandoning your King—your core values—then you will inadvertently confirm her beliefs about you

In this case, it is now the boy we mentioned above who speaks, not a worthy, reliable, and centered man. Any thoughts of harming her or yourself will tell you that this little boy is throwing a tantrum. Such thoughts originate from that immature and scared part of yourself. They expose you to the risk of appearing very weak. Any action under the influence of that little boy is a betrayal of your code of honor. The Warrior can accept difficult feelings as part of his journey. These hurt feelings make you human. Your vulnerability reveals nothing about your strengths or worthiness; only the way you manage it will.

The *Good Husband* will exercise his masculine strengths during such times of crisis. Even great Kings cry. They cry but stay on their thrones. Stay focused on what is most important in your life—your children, career, health, connection to people, and future dreams. Keep things in the perspective of time. Five or ten years from your current crisis, you will find yourself in a different relationship. The way you prove your resilience, decency, and care for your children during such a crisis will ultimately leave a lasting positive impact on your children and your self-esteem. It will turn out to be your sweet victory. I have seen it happen many times.

> ## PRACTICE:
>
> **If you have experienced threats, share with your wife what you learned here about their impact. Try to come to an agreement that you will both never use threats. Consult your Magician and consider constructive ways to express any emotional hurt.**

Slay the 'S' (shame) dragon

Both sexes use aggression on each other, but their methods are different. Males traditionally have used physical aggression that females cannot match. Instead, women tend to use their verbal and social skills to shame men. Shaming is not as lethal to the body but can cause serious mental hurt. Unlike physical aggression, you cannot see the bruises of shaming, so society can hardly trace and sanction it. When it happens behind closed doors, men are exposed to their vulnerable spots.

Just as we do not tolerate violence and intimidation against wives, we should stop tolerating messages of shame such as put-downs, humiliation, name-calling, criticism, and contempt against husbands. This form of aggression can be emotionally hurtful and damaging. Men must learn to combat this effectively.

But to stop this from happening, you have to be aware it's happening and call it out as shaming. Most of the time, men are out of touch with this feeling and fail to recognize the aggression that caused it. Their body is 'sinking,' but they fail to note what's going on. "It feels bad"—that's all they can say before they go quiet and withdraw. Next, they may burst with rage, or escape to alcohol or something else. This is where you need your Magician to notice your body sensations and the essential information they provide.

Precursors of shame are attacks on your personality rather than your behavior. Words such as "useless," "selfish," "idiot," or those exported from the cultural bug such as "chauvinist," "patriarchal," and "abusive" may trigger shame. They are aimed at your character, not your actions. They question your worth as a person. Spot the shaming energy of the message and call it out at once. Every single time! "This is shaming. Please don't turn on me like that." Don't argue with the content! Call out the toxic message and demand that your wife stop talking to you like that. Ask her to voice her needs or complaints without attacking you.

Shaming can be subtle, indirect, and hardly noticeable. It can be disguised as humor, gossip, and more. Many times you only realize the impact moments or hours later. It is absolutely okay if that's the case. But once you realize it, you have to call it out. As you learn to note it more often, the speed of your response will grow.

Women these days commonly use the term "unsafe" to assert their need to feel safe. You can use the term "shaming" to assert your need for acceptance and respect towards yourself.

"Share your feelings with me"

Women often want their partners to share feelings. This is in line with what society in general and therapists in particular expect men to do. The intention behind encouraging men to express their vulnerability this way is good. However, like many good intentions, it may lead a man to feel bad about himself if not done properly. I coach my male clients on knowing and sharing their feelings, but I am also very aware of how awkward this feels for many of them. It's as hard for tough men to express vulnerability as for insecure women to assert themselves. Both require sensitivity, acceptance, and patience.

A husband who is strong in his Warrior traits is likely also a good provider. Wives in these cases are happy with the good lifestyle that their men provide. But the men find themselves in a tragic trap! The very traits that make a man a successful provider (such as being dominant, competitive, tough, and a risk-taker) are often not compatible with emotional intimacy. Their love language of 'doing' clashes with the love language of 'being' that their wives may prefer to connect emotionally.

In the old days, when men did their hunting and fighting, their ancient brains learned to suppress vulnerability. The ability of these men to hold themselves together during painful or stressful tasks was a matter of survival. These same mechanisms are useful today for the tasks performed by pilots, surgeons, miners, builders, business people, and of course, those in the emergency and lifesaving fields.

The expectation to share your feelings may puzzle you. And if you attend couples therapy, you may also hear it from your therapist. Not only are you uncomfortable talking about your vulnerabilities, but you often don't even have the language for it. You end up feeling judged and inadequate. The too-familiar emotion of shame kicks in.

Well, sharing your feelings in intimate conversations is desirable but not an essential component of a healthy relationship. It is part of the social trend to shape men to fit a certain model of masculinity. Don't fall into the trap. Stay true to your masculine traits and don't feel guilt or shame about them. Deflect the pressure and expectation by saying "This is not my style… This is not me…" Honestly admit that sharing feelings is not your comfort zone. Once you set your boundary here, you can turn to what your wife ultimately seeks—connection. Suggest strengthening your connection in ways that are appealing to both of you. (See Chapter Five).

Throughout this book I have provided you with tools to authentically express how you feel and what you need to increase the chance of getting her to respond appropriately. This expression is different from women's heart-to-heart sharing with their girlfriends. This kind of intimate conversation and 'sharing feelings' is uncomfortable for most men I have known. Be assertive here and do not let anyone shame you if you are not into that kind of heart-to-heart conversation.

PRACTICE:

Share with your wife how shame works and its impact on you. Ask her to focus on your behaviors rather than your character if she needs to complain about something.

Explain to her how some of your reactions (such as withdrawal or anger) may result from shame, rather than you rejecting her.

Share your need to feel accepted and appreciated.

Protect your realm

Marital relationships may have external threats that cause conflict and undermine trust. Take for example the tension which commonly takes place between wives and their mothers-in-law. It is easy to blame the two women for the tension, but this often happens when a man creates a vacuum that sucks in both his mother's interventions and his wife's reactions. These dynamics say something about the man and his relationship with his mother. They are not a sign of maturity. As a Warrior you are supposed to have completed your separation from your mother. Either you need to mature yourself, or you need to set clear boundaries for her.

If your wife is the one who needs to fight with your mother, then this is destructive to all. It means that you do not do enough to protect your fortress. Her trust in you may be seriously damaged and the impact could surface years later.

And there is also the other side of this coin. Your wife could experience such high anxiety around your mother that she may try to prevent her from seeing her grandchildren. This will cause pain to your mother and may make you resent your wife.

Such family dynamics are another example of the price men pay for avoiding conflict and confrontation. Tap into your Warrior for help. Warriors don't blame others. They take responsibility for confronting issues and correcting such family situations. Use your Warrior energy to set clear boundaries for both your wife and your mother. They both need to know that you take charge. The message is not in what you say, but in the fact that you have a say. You are telling them that they are in your territory, and you are fully involved in what is happening. Address these issues as a Warrior—swiftly and with the desired results.

Your relationship fortress may also have threats from people who try to seduce either of you into activities that can risk your commitment and trust in each other. As a Warrior, you need to guard against such threats. Your denial of risks, disguised as 'openness' to your partner's explorations, will only open the gates for 'pests' who will destroy your 'garden.' Guard your garden. Don't shy away from clearly stating your concerns; even protest against certain activities or people you regard as threats. When partners do so, this is not 'controlling' but caring about the relationship. Partners want to feel how important they are to each other.

> ### PRACTICE:
>
> **Discuss with your wife the people or activities that cause tension between you.**
>
> **Agree on your approach toward such threats and the boundaries that will keep them away. Let her know how much you care about your bond.**

Swiftly end any aggressive episodes

As I described earlier, men are exposed to aggression and abuse in far greater numbers than those reported in the media. If you are in such a sad situation, you will need tools to address abusive episodes effectively. The commonly used passive-aggressive strategy of withdrawal only guarantees more anger and more attacks. Remember that women want their men to stay engaged. Her underlying message might mean—"I am desperately seeking your strength and support..." I remind you of the 'Hold Her' words of wisdom from the start of Chapter Three: "Hold her... Hold her when she is mad."

The meaning of her 'madness' can be understood in terms of her anxieties and vulnerability. She reacts to the intense pain that she cannot contain. Her reactivity is damaging her interests, but she doesn't realize that. She is losing you and she hates herself each time she acts aggressively. Many women with explosive and aggressive tempers suffer from a mental disorder known as borderline personality disorder (BPD).

The symptoms of BPD are linked to close relationships, as they stem from attachment wounds. Abandonment fears provoke strong reactivity that leads to unstable and volatile relationships. And if they believe their relationship is about to dissolve, some of these women can be dangerous to themselves or partners. They may threaten self-harm or embark on a journey of revenge and destruction towards their partners. (You can get an idea of what this looks like by watching YouTube videos from Johnny Depp's court case).

The term 'borderline' indicates that such people live on the border between reality and imagination. As such, they need a 'black and white' response. Any hesitation, arguing or vague response will fan their fire. Therefore, to effectively address the aggression, your response should be black and white. Make your 'border' very clear.

Your swift and clear response will help you both! Your wife will need your help to contain her rage, but you cannot help while you are under attack. You need to feel respected to support her. Your Magician will enable you to recognize that the rage is not about you. It is about her pain. Your Lover will enable you to feel for her and want to help her, and your Warrior will enable you to set clear boundaries to end any aggression towards you. It's crucial to see your partner's vulnerability in this situation and stay strong for your family as a whole. It is also imperative to end any aggression **at once**.

Aggressive episodes often end in court where the natural suspicion towards men makes it harder for them to gain justice. Over the years, quite a few men have needed my support in Family Court to gain custody or access to their children. The battle is never easy.

How to end aggressive episodes

As a Warrior, your way is action and engagement, not withdrawal. You command respect with your effective responses rather than protesting or complaining, and certainly not via victimhood.

Before we discuss Warrior strategies to assert yourself and command respect, I suggest keeping a few principles in mind.

The first is the principle of zero tolerance towards aggression. We can understand and accept feelings, but not certain behaviors. Feelings are always valid, including anger. Anger is valid in that it tells a personal story that carries some truth from the perspective of the angry person. When your wife feels hurt, powerless, or a sense of unfairness, you should respond with kindness by listening, trying to make sense of the situation, and offering support. But if she turns to you aggressively, you'll need to respond swiftly!

Aggression in a relationship starts like a small fire in the forest. It grows rapidly if it is not addressed swiftly. As this fire grows bigger, so does the cost and effort necessary to end it. Your wife may first blame you for an issue, then mumble a nasty word, then swear, then yell and so forth. Weak responses or avoidance in this situation only feed the fire. The principle is that the first time she attacks you, it is her fault; the second time is... well... still her fault. But from the third time, it becomes your fault. This third time should not arrive if you take on the responsibility to terminate it at once. This is not mathematics; it's an approach to work with.

As a Warrior, you are an agent of change which means you cannot be your wife's victim. You must be clear with your boundaries. Hesitation will come with a heavy price. A timely and strong response is crucial when it comes to aggression. Zero tolerance towards aggression should be the first principle for you and your wife.

Your second principle is to follow your 'shock' instincts. Imagine seeing an older child in the playground hitting your child. This will shock you, and this shock will instinctively drive you into action. This same instinct should apply when your wife hurts you. Reacting with numbness or indifference sends the wrong message. Your shock instinct sounds like: "Excuse me??" or "Did you just say **x**??" A response like one of these can often be enough to convey your message. To further drive your message home, ask her to promise you never again to be disrespectful towards you.

Your third principle is engagement. The movement of the Warrior is always forward in the direction of the goal. Avoidance weakens you. Disengagement in aggressive moments is toxic to your relationship with your wife **and** yourself. When you allow yourself to be poorly treated, everyone loses. Engagement means that you talk about what has happened and demonstrate your disapproval. Her aggression must **always** receive your strong disapproval. Your mission here is to encourage her to use new ways of expressing her anger. We don't seek control or defeat, but respect. Take it as your mission to coach your wife on authentic and respectful ways of expressing her hard feelings. I will show you how to do this in the remainder of this chapter

The fourth principle is the Warrior's code of using his strength in the service of his King (his values). Warriors only use their power to defend, not to assault weaker people. They are honorable. Attacking her should never be an option. Only losers act like that, not Warriors.

We will now look at a range of strategies you can use to end aggressive episodes swiftly.

The strategy of assertiveness

Assertiveness starts with having clarity about your basic right to feel free from any threat to your body, your dignity, your family, or your nation. Freedom from threats is how we experience our sense of respect. Assertiveness is a communication tool that helps us to live by this premise. It works in both directions—to command and to give respect.

Being assertive implies that you deal effectively with your fears. You are not afraid to say what you want, say no, change your mind, admit mistakes, etc. If for some reason you stop short of expressing your truth, you may react either with anger or with avoidance. You end up being aggressive, passive-aggressive (e.g., giving the silent treatment, being cynical), or passive. You weaken your voice and reduce the chance of getting people to respond to your needs.

The middle ground between being aggressive and passive is being assertive. You assert your voice. When you do so, your voice sounds clear, slow, and direct. People hear what you want or need. This is your authentic way. You don't hide, you don't suppress, and you don't attack. You share what is unconditionally valid and beyond judgment—your feelings and needs. You let the world know exactly what is going on for you. Telling someone "you are selfish" is not your truth, but your judgment and anger. The assertive way to convey the same message would be "It really disappointed me that you didn't help with that."

Assertiveness is power. Recall that we defined power as our ability to influence others. People don't have to respond to what you say, but by being assertive you increase the chance that they will take notice of you. You command respect by the very way you express yourself—being calm, brief, and direct. Others will listen when you do.

And do you know why they will listen? Because you have listened to yourself first! Let me explain.

The skill of assertiveness consists of two steps:

- Step 1 – notice your feelings and needs.
- Step 2 – communicate them to your partner.

The main challenges for people to be assertive are to read the cues in their body and name their feelings and needs. After all, how can people 'get you' if you don't tell them what you feel or need? Warriors don't let them guess. That would be playing the victim. Using "you" language and blaming each other escalates the cycle of attack-defend. Instead, Warriors take charge and alert others about their impact on them.

To be assertive, you need to enrich your emotional literacy. Language is the key and you will have to train yourself to speak in ways that may initially sound strange or feel uncomfortable for you. Here are a few examples:

- "I don't like it when you yell like that."
- "It doesn't feel right for me."
- "I am not comfortable with…"
- "It feels bad hearing you talking like that."
- "It worries me."
- "It really hurt."
- "I am disappointed."
- "I felt humiliated."
- "This felt absolutely awful."
- "I am shocked by how you turned on me."
- "This feels like shaming to me."
- "I am devastated."

Try to imagine a man who is not expressing these feelings. These unexpressed hurts may build resentment and rage, followed by outbursts of anger or passive-aggressive behaviors such as withdrawal. Failing to express is a loss of power. Being assertive enables you to reclaim your power.

When you state your request, it is essential to use a positive message. Express what you want or expect, rather than what you don't want. For example, instead of saying "don't talk to me like that," consider statements such as "talk to me with respect," "use softer language," "be kind," and "be more gentle." While engaging in such a conversation, always keep in mind the perspective I mentioned earlier: any aggression from your wife comes from her pain—her anxiety and powerlessness. The best response is for you to check what she needs and try to help.

The win/lose strategy

There could be moments when your wife's anger takes over and she doesn't respond to your requests to change the tone. Your only option in this situation is to disengage and move away. Obviously, such a move will further upset her, so you need to alert her gently about your intention. I call it the "win/lose" strategy. Make it clear how soft ways 'win' you, while aggressive ways 'lose' you. Reward her soft start-up with your positive attention and support. Be prepared to move away from her when she is aggressive.

As you gain experience with any of her aggressive episodes, you will be able to recognize the early signs. As soon as they appear, encourage her to "please start gently." Use positive words such as "slowly" and "softly." If she continues being aggressive, state calmly "you are losing me." If there is still no change, don't give her a third chance. Say "I am going to de-escalate the situation and take a little break before it's too late. Let's talk soon when we are both calm," and then move out of the room or out of the house. This may lead to a bigger storm in the short-term, but after a few times, she will hopefully understand what "losing you" means. As a true Warrior, you don't turn this strategy into another passive-aggressive tactic. The goal is not to punish your wife, but to defend yourself from aggression.

The first time you use this strategy, she may explode with rage. When you come back you need to remind her of your response to aggression—"I will do exactly the same the next time you attack me. Start gently and you win me; start aggressively and you lose me." Keep using hints such as "gently," "slowly," and then "you are losing me" every single time she turns to you aggressively. And if she does turn gently, make her a Queen—always listen and try to respond to her needs.

A man with a soft hand

Bob tried talking to calm his wife down, but it didn't work. One day he discovered that using body language was more effective than just him talking. As soon as she started to raise her voice, he hinted softly to her with his hand like you would do to tell other drivers to slow down. While moving his hand, he said "gently please... gently please" in a soft voice. He didn't engage with his wife's words, and he didn't react. He kept calm while trying to lower her tone. After a few instances, she started to respond well to his hints.

But what if your wife refuses to talk?

Some aggressive women refuse to talk about their aggression because they are too ashamed of their behavior and won't admit mistakes. They say, "I don't want to talk about it," when their husbands try to discuss their hurt. Such a strategy leaves these men feeling dismissed and frustrated. Not only because they have been attacked and hurt, but because there is not even room for them to be heard.

So, how can you address the issue if she refuses to talk? You don't fight with her. Instead, suspend your response until the next time she turns to you. It might be in a few moments or a few hours. When she does, remind her that your previous conversation has not finished yet. Don't move on to her agenda. Stay with your agenda! Hold your ground and make sure that the next interaction will be only to discuss what happened. Make sure that she listens and you should expect some resolution or apology.

The strategy of accountability

I discussed the strategy of accountability in Chapter Four on the King. I encourage you to go over it again if you need to end aggressive episodes. People who repeat aggressive behaviors in relationships must be held accountable by their partners. It is absolutely not enough to say "sorry." It is your responsibility to hold your wife to account if she attacks you. If she is genuine about her intention to stop her aggression, then she should accept the accountability exercise as a tool to help her change her behavior.

Have an accountability conversation with her and ask her to agree on the consequences if she acts aggressively and hurts you. Encourage her to choose the kind of consequence that best serves her learning. The idea is not to punish, only to do what a mature person does to take responsibility and correct a mistake. In my experience, partners are often short of ideas for what can be a suitable consequence, so let me suggest some here:

- She leaves her mobile phone with you for a few hours.
- She takes it upon herself to complete a chore she doesn't enjoy.
- She texts you her apology.
- She cannot do one of her hobbies for some time.

The written response strategy

I explained why a written message is a powerful tool in Chapter Six. This tool can be particularly useful in cases of aggression. The following letter was sent by one of my clients to his wife after years of emotional and physical abuse. Her explosive temper scared him so badly that talking to her was too intimidating an option for him. It took some time for him to gain the courage to share his feelings with her via email. It was safer for him to produce an effective message using my guidance.

Dear Cathy

I have been thinking a lot about our relationship, and I wanted to share with you my thoughts and feelings. I prefer writing to you because it allows me to choose my words carefully and I also want to make sure that you hear me. When I try talking to you I end up feeling attacked. My hope with this letter is that you understand my experience and consider other ways to express your frustrations.

Over the last few years your anger and outbursts of aggression have escalated to a point that I can no longer tolerate. I know you are in pain but the way you express it makes me move away from you. I know it hurts you even more but I am not sure how to protect myself from your rage, swearing, and putdowns, or when you throw things at me. Your threats hurt me and humiliate me in front of our two girls.

The unpredictable outbursts are scary and they worry me. I feel terribly hurt and I am worried about our girls. Up until now I was not sure what to do, but this is going to change. I can't take it any more.

Counseling has helped me reflect on my values, on what really is important to me, to us, and to our girls. I can now see that I have been sacrificing my most important values such as self-respect, authenticity, safety for us all, and care for our girls. When I tolerated your aggression I betrayed these values.

My fears got in the way. I didn't want to risk our relationship and our family life. It was my mistake that I allowed you to treat me badly for too long.

I need to let you know that from now on I will show zero tolerance towards any form of aggression. I will use any reasonable means to stop that, including Police, intervention order or separation. Every legal option will be on the table.

The person you present at home is very different to who you present as a nurse at work. I am not sure why. Your aggression is not who you are, not the person I love. But a kind of disease we must treat urgently if we want to stay together. I see that you're suffering, and I hope you get some help. I am here to help you because I care about you and our family.

I am afraid that with more aggression towards me you are going to lose me. All I hope is to be treated with respect even when I am not at my best. I am open to any help from a third party if you wish.

What do you think?

Yours

Peter

The impact of this letter was dramatic. She protested calmly and then went quiet for a few days. He later discovered that she had started to take medication. The aggression stopped at once!

The mirror strategy

Women are more cautious than men about expressing aggression in public. The feminine persona on display to the public is usually of a soft and kind person. This façade is critical for the social approval women seek. Their aggression can be a taboo among their female communities, just as displaying vulnerability can be taboo for the masculine persona.

Aggressive women often avoid couples therapy because it puts them in a vulnerable position and embarrasses them to hear their husbands sharing how they behave at home. We need to be careful with this method because we know how hurtful shaming is. Yet, you can use her own consciousness as her internal 'public eyes.' You only need to put her behaviors before her eyes for her to see herself in the mirror. Facing her aggressive behavior will confront her façade of kindness.

Men rarely share domestic violence against them with the outside world. They would rather keep it private. Well, if you don't share with anyone then the very least you can do is take the case of your wife's aggression to… her! Let **her** know how bad and hurtful her behavior is. The act of mirroring means that you make her aware of how she sounds or looks. One of my clients used his mobile phone to openly record his wife's aggressive behavior and then played it back to her. She was embarrassed.

Text message

Rob used to text his partner the very nasty words that she had just said to him. It proved a powerful exercise. Her aggression was now documented on their mobile phones and could be referred to. During a couples session, Rob shared the messages on his mobile. There was a moment of quiet embarrassment. After that, we were able to have an open conversation about her pain. Once the demons were out of the basement, we could start a healing process. Rob's partner became aware of her pain, and was more cautious and considerate with her language.

Prepare for the battle over your children

I wish I didn't need to write this segment of the chapter.

Sadly, sometimes you need your combative Warrior if your relationship is on the path to divorce. I assume that if you read a book like this one, you see yourself as a man who tried to do good for his family. However, no matter how good you are as a husband, it is not a guarantee that your relationship is working well, nor that your wife is someone you can reason with.

For whatever reason, your relationship may not end amicably. Influenced by her lawyers and the cultural bug, your wife may get increasingly combative as you proceed through the legal process of separation. Denying any risks or playing the nice guy may harm your interests in this situation. You will have to be wise and prepare yourself. Under the influence of the cultural bug, terms such as 'domestic violence' and 'abusive relationship' may be pushed and used against you. The Family Court environment these days doesn't favor men. You will need to fight for your future relationship with your children.

This fight should begin with the first signs of danger. If she ever calls you "abusive," it should be a red flag to you. This might be her first 'bullet' in a custody battle. If it is, huge waves are coming your way. To avoid highly popular fault accusations being made against you, I advise documenting all communication and interaction with her. For example, letters or text messages. If nothing else, your documentation may deter her and her lawyers from taking a dirty path. I suggest it as a defensive move, not as a manipulative strategy.

I routinely challenge my male clients to do their best for their families, but when they are abused by their wives or at risk of losing contact with their children, I become their 'lawyer.' Over the years quite a few men have needed my support in Family Court to gain custody or access to their children. Men's battle for justice in Family Court can be tough in the current climate. They need advocacy, and I hope to see more male and female professionals join this advocacy mission.

Takeaway messages to activate your Warrior

Activate your Warrior to command and restore respect towards you. Your Warrior is the energy most linked to the traditional male roles of being the provider and protector. Your capacities and strengths as a Warrior are what your wife needs the most while raising your young children. Of the four roles in our *Good Husband* model, your performance in this role will prove most crucial to how she respects and appreciates you. Your Warrior energy will help you to accomplish goals, provide for your family, protect your realm, and assert your boundaries.

Your action plan

- Learn the Warrior way and code. Take pride in your masculine traits. Despite the cultural attack on masculinity, these traits are highly demanded by women.

- Mobilize your anger to serve you as your fuel in the fight for the safety of your family and to command respect.

- Engage constructively in conflicts rather than attacking or withdrawing. Aim for solutions, not to be 'right.'

- Fulfill your mission as a provider. It goes to the heart of your identity as a man and as a Warrior.

- Take care of yourself, and build your own social network of male friends.

- Deal with divorce threats effectively and don't let any fear of losing her compromise your self-respect.

- Call out any attempts to shame you and convey a strong message to stop them.

- Take a proactive stance towards any external threat to your marriage or to your wife. Protect your territory.

- Swiftly end any aggressive episode and show zero tolerance towards aggression.

- Prepare yourself for a battle over your children once you recognize the danger signs of an upcoming dirty war.

8
MANAGING CONFLICTS
– A CASE STUDY

"Despite what many therapists will tell you, you don't have to resolve your major marital conflicts for your marriage to thrive... Problems are inevitably part of a relationship. We may not love these problems, but we are able to cope with them, avoid situations that worsen them, and develop strategies and routines that help us deal with them."

— **John Gottman and Nan Silver,** *The Seven Principles for Making Marriage Work*

"It is that fear of emotional disengagement that precipitates the demands, criticism, arguments, and silences that mark troubled couples... Conflict is almost always an attempt to call a partner back into emotional connection."

— **Sue Johnson, Love Sense**

Marital conflicts are normal and universal. They change in frequency and intensity during marriage. Conflicts and disagreements do not have to harm your relationship. In fact, at least two- thirds of the problems that partners argue about are perpetual. That is, partners learn to live with them without a clear resolution. We know this from the research on couples who have stayed together for many years.[97] What matters is how partners approach these conflicts. If they are not handled constructively, conflicts can leave a lasting impact of resentment and damaged trust. This impact often surfaces in unpredictable times and contexts, leaving partners puzzled by what seems to be an overreaction. Therefore, managing conflict is a burning issue for couples to get it right.

Marital conflicts are uniquely difficult because they provoke your deepest fears. As I have suggested a few times in this book—blame your attachment brain for that. Attachment is a biological mechanism. It makes us seek the closeness of another human being for the purpose of survival. We gradually develop trust and we want to feel secure. The threat of separation, betrayal or abandonment by our attachment figure provokes intense anxiety. The brain interprets each of these actions as threats to our survival and activates the fight or flight response. As a result, the stress hormone floods the body.

This primal attachment mechanism gets to work when you fall in love. As soon as that happens, the fear of losing your partner kicks in. You are wired to need her care. You expect your partner to be there unconditionally even during conflicts. You trust her never to abandon you. Yet in most cases, your partner is not as safe as your parents (hopefully) were.

Themes of conflict, such as child-rearing, money, and sex, are eternal and largely passion-driven. Yet, the ways of resolving these conflicts have changed dramatically and partners in our modern culture are challenged in quite a few ways.

First, the idea of intimacy is new in evolutionary terms. Men and women have traditionally done things with their mates, but now they rely on each other as the primary support. The gender differences that appear stronger than ever during the phase of child-rearing are hard to navigate. The ideals of intimacy and friendship hardly 'sync' with the harsh reality. Needs are not easy to meet during this phase, so there is an ongoing sense of disappointment and subtle grief, which taints the goodwill required for settling differences peacefully.

Second, the ever-present questions of power and justice instill doubts and confusion in partners about their respective roles and the division of tasks. They may approach conflicts as yet another form of struggle for power without clear rules or processes for negotiating solutions. They often feel powerless and trapped during conflicts.

Third, the option of separation is evoked with ever increasing speed and lightness. Sadly, many partners are too blind to see the terrible ramifications of that. Conflicts ring the alarm bells in their attachment brain with more urgency, resulting in an intense reactivity to them. When conflicts take place on the edge of the abyss of divorce, no wonder they escalate so quickly. Rather than conflicts being perceived as something natural, an authentic clash of needs, and even a growth enhancer, they are seen as a threat to the very survival of the marriage.

As you can see, conflicts expose the tragic impact of the gap between nature and nurture—the gap between our ancient instincts, and the voice of culture. Nature speaks of the need for security and commitment, while culture speaks of individualism and the search for happiness. One says 'overcome hardships for the sake of security to all' and the other says 'if it's too difficult, separate for the sake of your happiness.' The voice of culture is tragically misunderstood and misused in the context of raising a family, but in the cultural bug climate, merely discussing the negative consequences can be seen as 'old-fashioned,' 'traditional,' and even 'chauvinist.'

One thing is clear though. Resolving conflicts in a fair and satisfying manner is very complex in modern marriage. Getting the formula right is a matter of urgency for partners today. You both require good skills to navigate conflicts effectively. It is a work of art.

Do men respond differently to conflicts than women?

Yes. Men both perceive and respond differently to conflicts than women. The classic pattern is that women pursue/demand while men withdraw/avoid. Conflicts with intimate partners confront men and expose their vulnerability for several reasons:

- First, when responding to stress, women tend to seek connection and want to talk, but men tend to do the exact opposite. Men's natural reaction of taking time and space to recover may be seen by their partners as avoiding them, or worse.

- Second, in their ancient instincts, conflict for men means either losing or winning. Take out the sword and fight. The idea of negotiating needs and goals is new to our savage brains. It requires a verbal set of skills, not a physical set.

- Third, settling differences through talking taps into female verbal abilities. Men who struggle to articulate thoughts and feelings may find themselves disadvantaged. They just want to get to the solution. To avoid further arguments, some men may prefer to let their wives get what they want at the expense of their voices and interests. It is obviously not a sustainable long-term solution.

- Fourth, conflicts have traditionally been resolved according to hierarchy, as in the workplace. The person in charge has the final say. In the modern family we are equal, which means that the process is unknown and unpredictable. For many men, such an environment undermines their ability to function with clarity and resolve.

- Fifth, men tend to prefer the idea of serving and protecting their wives, rather than fighting them. Their wives are their main driving force for proving their Warrior capacities. But what do you do if your wife turns from being your object of protection to becoming a source of threat?

As you can see, when it comes to resolving marital conflicts, the ancient version of masculinity is not user-friendly in a modern family. This is partly why men are losing power in marriage. Women keep empowering themselves with assertive expression of what they need. They have long moved away from the traditional role of obedient and submissive wives. Good for them! And how do men match that? To restore their power during conflicts, men need to modernize their masculine application for resolving conflicts. The four masculine roles can help you accomplish that. Let's see how.

Managing conflicts using your masculine roles

Let's get imaginative for a moment and invite each of the characters to stand on stage and give a speech on the 'How I manage conflicts' topic. This will illustrate how you (as the 'casting director') can bring a certain character to life and use its masculine strengths in the context of your marital conflicts.

The King's speech

"As a King, I maintain order during conflicts. My responsibility is to keep a healthy system that manages our conflict constructively. I make sure we stick to our values and abide by our family rules so that we serve our family. I always keep the big picture in my mind. Whatever we argue about, I always remember the overall vision of staying close and together. When conflicts escalate, I act like the boat's captain during stormy weather—I drop the anchor to keep us stable. I don't get bogged down in endless arguing, but seek a win-win solution instead.

"I understand that conflicts are a normal part of life and I welcome differences as a sign that we are free to express our passions and desires. We clash from time to time and that is okay. It is a sign that we are fully alive and fully expressed. My goal is not harmony, but a constructive process of honest sharing of what we need. I hope to settle our differences so that we are both satisfied. I know that most conflicts are not resolvable, so I look for ways to adapt and compromise.

"As a leader, I take a proactive and preventative approach. I know that bitter fights result from a loss of connection rather than a petty issue we fight about. I nourish our friendship and closeness to guarantee a softer tone during conflicts. I organize activities that bring us closer and enrich our emotional bank account.

"As King and Queen, we rule our family with 'laws.' I negotiate using these agreements and rules. More chaos means more conflicts, while more order means more security and peace. I bring order to areas where we often argue, such as house chores, disciplining the kids, spending money, etc. If a conflict occurs, I think of ways to minimize the risk of it happening again. Our 'book of laws' is evolving continuously. We develop our unique culture of how we do things in our family.

"If we get stuck in an unproductive cycle of arguing, I consider using a third party: a counselor, priest/rabbi, or a family member. I do not want us to suppress and resign with a sense of unfairness, as this is a recipe for growing resentment.

"I am aware of the deep-seated fears that conflicts can provoke and how we both risk 'losing it.' My goal as a King during such tense moments is to stick to the no-hurt principle— 'there shall be no hurt.' I check that we follow it religiously. We never leave any 'injuries' behind. I evoke our values through statements such as 'let's keep calm,' 'stay respectful please,' and 'I remind you about kindness.' I never retaliate. If she gets aggressive, I remove myself and show my disapproval through my sadness."

The Lover's speech

"As a lover, I can sense my unpleasant feelings and body sensations during conflicts, but I choose to remain engaged. I don't defend, attack, or withdraw. I am hurting and she is hurting as well. Conflicts make us both sad and worried because during those moments we are not aligned or close to each other. To repair our rupture, I try to reconnect to her.

"I use the language of the heart to express what I feel and need. I remain open and allow her to see my hurts and vulnerability. I speak the authentic voice of my heart instead of using inauthentic control strategies such as threats, anger, blame, or passive-aggressiveness. I let her know if I felt sad or hurt or worried.

"I listen to her pain and I validate her concerns. I respond with "I see..." or "I hear..." to show her that I 'get' her. I don't let shame drive me away from the situation or get defensive. I stay connected.

"I am willing to take ownership and acknowledge any mistake I have made that has contributed to the conflict. I say sorry. I assume she wants to forgive me and move on, and that she needs me to express some apology.

"I know that after a fight we both hurt and feel like withdrawing from each other. As a Lover, this time is the ultimate test of my love. I reach out and I offer to reconnect. I take charge of the repair. I sense how difficult it is for her to recover from her hurt feelings. I may offer her a hug to help her calm down. I want us both to bounce back after a rupture. I show how much I care about us as a family."

The Magician's speech

"As a Magician, I am most needed during conflicts because this is when reactivity runs high. My capacity for non-reactive responses is tested the most when conflicts provoke our strong emotions. I intensify my alertness. I know that our attachment brain is speaking in these moments. We are confronted by ghosts from the past—by threats of separation and abandonment. Panic might kick in. I am aware our fears may confront and anger us both. The risk of saying hurtful things or acting badly is at its peak. In these moments, I try to observe and examine what is happening here and now. I try to make sense of our feelings. I know that reactivity can escalate the conflict, so I deliberately slow down.

"During conflict I am mindful of any strong reaction in my body. I am aware of signs of tension, shame, or anxiety. I self-soothe. I slow my breathing. I note to myself how quickly my body tensed up. I pay attention to my body. I inhabit my body when it tenses up, rather than moving away from it. I exercise self-regulation.

"I am aware of how our filter can stir things up. If we are hurt and worried, our red filter makes us more pessimistic. We may generalize ("you always…, we never…, we don't suit each other…") or personalize ("he is selfish …, she is hysterical…, I am a failure"). I look for possible assumptions and interpretations that create or intensify the conflict. I try to identify subconscious beliefs that are hardly noticeable and act as mental bugs. These beliefs may come from past experiences of powerlessness, rejection, betrayal, exploitation, or abuse. For example, "this is the end," "I'm being victimized again," "I'm being controlled," "I am not loved," "I will be punished," or "I am failing."

"When she says something that sounds outrageous, I try to stay curious. I don't race to conclusions or assumptions. I ask "what is happening?" and "what does it mean?" Asking and wondering is an effective way to stay non-reactive. I respond by giving the benefit of the doubt. There is something here I need to understand better. As hidden storytellers, our conflicts tell us something about what matters to us so much. I want to explore and understand whether it is about justice, connection, or something else.

"I am aware of how the demand/withdraw cycle works and I try to avoid it. I see the first signs, such as complaints or blame, and I choose a different response. If my past reaction was withdrawal, I now choose to stay engaged. I make us both aware that we are stepping into a cycle of reactivity. I will suggest trying something different.

"When we are both caught in a heated conversation, I know the danger of being reactive. I suggest a timeout to de-escalate. "Let's take a break and continue later?" I will ensure we get back to the topic within a reasonable time.

"I adopt an optimistic perspective and look at conflicts through a 'green' filter. I do not see them as a threat or a battle to win or lose, but as an opportunity to learn and grow. We evolve and change continuously as we negotiate our needs and desires. Clashes of needs or values signify that we are alive and fully expressed.

"I accept that many of our differences are never resolved. I accept and embrace them as part of life. I learn to let go. I also remember that we have overcome many conflicts before. I know we are resilient. If the crisis is serious, I keep in mind that many couples like us have gone through big crises and not only stayed together, but come out of them stronger."

The Warrior's speech

"As a Warrior, I operate with a code of honor. I ensure we stay respectful and don't hurt each other, even when we are angry. I accept frustration and anger as valid emotions. Protesting and complaining are okay, but I show zero tolerance towards aggression. When she kindly requests anything from me, I try to serve her as my Queen, but if she attacks me, she will lose me. I will demand to be treated with respect before she can get what she needs from me.

"I set clear boundaries if I need to. I communicate what I want assertively. I do not try to appease or please in order to be liked or avoid conflict. Our goal during conflict is to get what we both want. I try to resolve it fairly and with mutual consideration. I listen.

"I do not avoid difficult conversations even if language may not be a strong skill of mine. Conflicts with my wife expose my vulnerabilities and make me uncomfortable, yet as a Warrior I respond with courage and resilience. I face my fears and I stay engaged.

"I seek action and a solution. I am not interested in endless arguments about who is right or wrong. I cut short victimhood stories about the past. I don't play the victim and I don't complain. With my sense of agency, I want to know what to do to resolve the conflict. I may say "okay, just tell me what you want." When possible and reasonable, I will act instantly to make her happy.

"If she threatens separation, I ask her never to use such threats again because they are a form of emotional abuse. I tell her I am open to working on our issues but that if she wants to separate, she should contact a lawyer and let me know. As a Warrior, I can cope with the challenge of separation. I am resilient and able to manage my life if I need to live on my own again. I will make sure that my kids are protected and well looked after by both of us."

Your takeaway messages

Conflicts present a difficult challenge to partners in modern families because they expose the innate gap between our ancient instincts and culture-driven expectations. Men need to modernize their masculine applications for resolving conflicts. Each of the masculine roles presents some possibilities:

- As the King, you focus on maintaining order. That is, the values, rules, and big picture of your life together as a family. You make sure you both don't break the rules.
- As the Lover, you tend to her pain and needs, and you try to understand her and offer support.
- As the Magician, you adopt a non-reactive attitude to guarantee your conflicts do not escalate.
- As the Warrior, you do not avoid the conflict; you engage with it instead. You try to find a practical solution to satisfy you both. If attacked, you set boundaries and command respect.

9
FATHERHOOD

"That is the thankless position of the father in the family: the provider for all, and the enemy of all."

— **J. August Strindberg**

"If there is any immortality in us human beings, it is certainly only in the love that we leave behind. Fathers like mine don't ever die."

— **Leo Buscaglia**

We love our role as fathers, and our community loves to see us in this role. Fatherhood is one of the more noble ways to turn our masculine energy into a constructive, purposeful, and creative power. The mission is compelling, consuming, and filled with meaning. For me, becoming a father was the most transformative moment in my life. It went straight to the core of my identity. I suddenly felt a strong sense of purpose and direction.

The new status meant I had an important role to fulfill in society. This role was my unquestionable right, but also a huge responsibility. I became a King—'Everything I do from now on is for my kingdom.' It came with an immense sense of clarity and focus. The irreversibility of becoming a parent made me feel centered. No one can sack me from this position. My mind could no longer dream wildly, and my desires had to converge into a single mission—taking care of my family. I also felt an opportunity to provide my kids with a very different environment from the one I had as a child. It turned out to be a healing experience for my childhood wounds. Indeed, children represent hope in so many ways.

Most men would relate to this experience and proudly live up to their dream of being a good father. The young fathers I see around me—my nephews and my clients—are totally dedicated to their families and deeply involved in the lives of their children. They deserve our appreciation and support.

Do they get any of that?

Quite the opposite. Acknowledgment and admiration for the challenging job of parenting are routinely given to mothers, while fathers seem to be taken for granted. Demonstrating that special love for your mother will surely score points in the eyes of the public. This is a good trick that many politicians and celebrities do to boost their public image. And when it comes to the media or family court, the picture is pretty bleak.

In their seminal book *The Boy Crisis*, scholars Warren Farrell and John Gray argue that society wages war against fathers. Farrell and Gray present a powerful case for fatherhood reflecting on the many children who grow up without fathers. With data from countries worldwide, they illustrate a clear picture of how fathers matter for the well-being of their children: the highly detrimental impact of absent fathers versus the immense benefits of engaged fathers. Furthermore, when raised in single parent families, research suggests that boys and girls fare better if the parent is the father![98]

Yet, there are some hopeful signs of a change in attitude towards the role of fathers. Canada, for example, started a few programs to support fathers in 2008.[99] Policy-makers and researchers there have begun to adopt a new way of thinking about fathers both within and apart from their families, and as cultural groups. Fathers are increasingly acknowledged, supported, and honored for their unique contributions to their children and families.[100] Knowing how men find purpose in their parental roles, it should not surprise us that fatherhood also comes with health benefits for men.[101]

Seeing fathers at their best and how children flourish with them was a key motivation for writing this book. I wanted to help fathers improve their marital skills to increase the chances of their kids growing up in secure and supportive families. As we often see, when something is not working well in a marriage, the fatherhood project is at risk. Sadly, too many children pay a heavy price for that. In the US and UK, one in three children grows up without an involved father.[102]

Your fathering role is highly contingent on your wife's mothering role and your relationship with her. Therefore, it is essential to maintain a healthy relationship with your wife, as this book guides you. You can be a good father, but not quite a *Good Husband*. But if you are a *Good Husband*, you are also a good father because you provide your children with what they need the most—satisfied parents and a stable family.

Changes in how the role of fatherhood is perceived

Your role is not at all straightforward. Like masculinity, fatherhood is constantly shaped by cultural changes. It requires conscious learning and adaptation. Motherhood on the other hand is driven by biological processes and is mostly shaped by nature.

Your perception of your role as a father is forever in the making. In the old days, your role was to provide and protect. You may sense the echo of your ancient instincts in your desire to focus on work and relax when you come home. However, today the expectations are that you equally share the responsibility for household chores and parenting tasks with your wife. The fatherhood role perception has moved from being a breadwinner, disciplinarian, or assistant to the mother, to sharing parenting or even being the primary caregiver in some cases. This kind of fully involved fatherhood is an integral part of what makes *The Good Husband*.

Fatherhood and motherhood

Evolution has designed different missions for mothers and fathers. Your wife's feminine capacities are tailored for the survival of vulnerable babies—for nurturing and caring. Your masculine capacities are tailored for functioning successfully in the world so that you can provide and protect. Your respective natural capacities as female and male complement each other in your parenting roles. Her loving responses towards your children are aimed at providing security. They naturally reinforce closeness and dependency.

The mission of the masculine is to facilitate the process of children moving away from their secure base towards individuation and independent coping with their surrounding world. While your wife lays the foundation for a sense of worthiness, belonging, and security in your children, you lay the foundation for their competence, resilience, and accomplishments. She provides the building blocks and you provide the 'gym' where your children prepare themselves to adjust to the 'real' world and meet the challenges of independent life. Your wife teaches your children self-love, while you teach them self-directedness. That is, to be the agent who takes responsibility for your child's life. (In some families, these masculine/feminine roles can be reversed).

Based on these role differences, it is sensible to gradually build your fatherhood role to match your child's developmental needs. In the early stage of babyhood, your wife and baby are inseparable. Therefore, your best service to your child is to be responsive to what your wife says or wants. As your child begins the process of individuation and exploration of the world, your direct involvement becomes increasingly important for their growth.

Since very young children don't clearly articulate what they need, your wife's motherhood instincts give her an advantage during this stage. It's wise to accept this natural advantage with humility rather than avoiding your child or getting frustrated. Let her lead. You can be an excellent playmate. Your disciplinarian role will begin to take shape when your child is about three.

Around the age of eight when your child is able to reason, you should begin to discuss rules and consequences. Your importance in their life will grow significantly during adolescence and peak as they reach adulthood when they are less interested in the 'security' that their mother offers. In fact, they may often get annoyed by your wife's nurturing behaviors because it clashes with their desire to grow towards independence and autonomy. As they prepare for a life out of the home, they increasingly seek your guidance and company. So be patient and optimistic during the childhood phase. Unleashing your full potential as a father is 'yet to come.'

The father effect

There is growing evidence of the importance of fathers for their children's development and well-being. This is known as the father effect. The Canadian Father Involvement initiative mentioned earlier in this chapter reads as a compelling case for boosting the role of fathers in the life of their children.[103]

Children of involved fathers tend to fare better in the following areas:

- Cognitively, they demonstrate more competence and better academic achievements, and they reach higher levels of educational achievement and career success.
- Psychologically, they are often more stable and resilient, and suffer less mental health issues. They show more tolerance for frustration, and are better able to take the initiative and use self-direction and self-control. As young adults, they experience greater life satisfaction.
- Socially, they get along with friends, respect rules, and adjust better to the environments of school and work.

In sum, the quality of the father/child relationship is the variable most consistently associated with positive life outcomes.

By comparison, children who grow up without a father are more likely to:

- suffer from poorer impulse control,
- have a weaker sense of right and wrong, and
- have troubled relationships with their peers.

During adolescence, boys without a father engage more in antisocial behaviors and take drugs. Teenage girls without a father take more risks with their sexuality, with terrible potential consequences such as becoming a victim of rape or pregnancy. Farrell says: "The lack of father involvement is the single most predictor of suicide; it is one of the biggest predictors of a child not graduating high school, dropping out of school."[104]

But what do we mean when we say "involved father"?

There are three components to being an involved father.

1. Time

   You spend time with your children. You are available and accessible. You are present and active during their home activities. You play with them.

2. Relating

   You are warm, close, affectionate, supportive, encouraging, and accepting. Your child is attached to you and feels secure with you. They turn to you in time of need.

3. Balanced role

   You act on both aspects of your parental role—providing discipline **and** support. You set boundaries, enforce consequences, and show care and sensitivity towards your child's needs. You balance the feminine and masculine energies.

Parenting by using your masculine strengths

Let's turn now to our *Good Husband* model (of King, Lover, Magician, and Warrior) and see how it can be used to boost your fatherhood capacities.

The father King

As a father King, you respond to your children with the future in mind. This is how leaders operate—they begin at the end, with the vision. A mother's strength is in her sensitivity and responsiveness to what is unfolding at the present moment. Her instincts 'know' what to do. They are spontaneous. They happen organically from bottom-up processes, and from what emerges in your child's behavior in the here and now.

You balance your wife's instincts with your top-down capacity. You lead with the big picture in mind, considering what's beyond the present moment. You operate from the conscious level of the intentions and values of your family.

Your chaotic, vulnerable children will be a constant challenge for her. At times, it can be confusing and emotionally overwhelming for her. Children's intense emotions are unpredictable and may provoke anxiety. Your wife and kids need security from you, and you provide it by creating order. As the head of order in your family, you need to make your family members aware of your important values such as kindness, respect towards you and your wife as parents, self-discipline, and more. Embrace your fatherhood role of family authority with love and a profound sense of responsibility. It is not an easy role. You cannot expect to be liked for it, not even by your wife, even though she should understand the importance of your role on a logical level.

Always use your father King authority to serve the best interests of your family. This motivation is crucial to both how you embrace your role and how your family perceives you. Lead by using respect and love rather than intimidation and aggression. You are less likely to resort to harsh methods when you rely on the power of your King's 'crown'—your system, principles, and rules. Your voice represents the common good of the family rather than your ego. Your authority enforces the 'way'—the values of your family, not a whim of the moment. When you instruct your kids, they will be able to tell whether it's a whim or you are using the voice of your 'crown.'

The voice of the father King sounds slow, short, and serious, without yelling. When you speak like that, your kids can tell that you mean what you say. And as they learn to trust your words, they will come to honor what you say. If you are committed to your 'way,' they will gradually follow it. Your kids will flourish in such a secure and predictable environment. You can reasonably predict the positive impact on both their mother and your marital relationship.

As a King, you care about the authority of both parents in your family. The authority role may not come easily for your wife. At times, particularly as they approach adolescence, you might need to coach your kids to treat their mother as a Queen—an authority who deserves their respect. If they dismiss or ignore her, step in to demand respect on behalf of the 'crown.' Always back her up.

You are right to expect her to back you up as well, but disappointingly, too often her motherly reactivity may get in her way so that she takes on the role of a rescuer. (More on that later.) As you now understand, 'double standards' are not a curse but just how we adjust to our different strengths and vulnerabilities as males and females.

Enforcing boundaries will always attract some protest from your children, but as a King you can see what is best for them in the long run. Research on child development is behind you. The authoritative parenting style is best for your children compared to the authoritarian (rigid control), indulgent, and uninvolved styles.[105] The authoritative parenting style provides the right balance between responsiveness and demandingness. In other words, the masculine tendency to challenge and confront balances the feminine tendency to nurture and support. Ideally, each of you will balance the masculine/feminine within yourself and exhibit both boundaries and warmth.

As a leader, try to teach and inspire. Be proactive, not reactive. Always use positive language describing the desirable behavior from your children. Policing will make you use negative language, while leadership uses positive language. Your expectations and intentions will be very influential on your children's minds, so tell them what you expect of them. Develop the habit of saying "Do" instead of "Don't." "Go slowly" instead of "Don't go wild." "Treat your sister kindly" instead of "Don't push her." "Speak with respect" instead of "Don't be rude."

Good leaders also take a preventative approach. They learn from their past mistakes and employ strategies to prevent them from happening again. Rather than putting out fires, you want to foresee and prevent them instead. Put rules in place to prevent bad behaviors by your children. Reward desirable behaviors by using encouraging words. Let your children know how happy or proud you are when they behave well.

As you exercise your authority, keep the cultural bug in mind. Your role as a masculine authority figure is under constant attack. Don't be surprised if you suddenly hear from your wife that you act like a tyrant, patriarch, or something else. Such a comment may rightly irritate you. If it happens, consult your Warrior to command respect. As an authentic King who is focused not on your ego but on how best to serve your family, simply remind your wife of the 'way'—the big picture and why you exercise your authority. Speak less and do more. Don't let the cultural bug noise get in your way.

Mistakes of the father King

Recall that each masculine role has two extreme ends. Watch out for being an overactive King—one who is authoritarian, controlling, and punitive. And be similarly wary of being an underactive King—abdicating your throne and showing no interest in any leadership or disciplinarian role with your children.

This underactive King is far more common today. Some men find it convenient for their wives to take care of everything in the family while they settle for the traditional role of being the provider and 'assistant' to the mothers.

The father Lover

As a father Lover, you focus on your children's feelings and needs. We usually see a gap between mothers and fathers in this area. Mothers are more attuned to their children's feelings. Your wife's sensitivity and responsiveness are her unique female gifts. But you may often find yourself frustrated because you cannot make sense of what your child wants. The result may be abrupt and impatient responses from you. These responses may upset both your child and your wife. Understanding your child will require some intention and conscious effort. It means wondering "What do they need?"

It is particularly challenging when children are young and not verbal. Fathers mostly dislike second guessing. For the masculine to operate comfortably, he needs clear directions, as in a manual. However, clear communication is a matter of development in children. As they grow in their ability to talk and reason, the task should become easier for you. Your fatherhood role evolves over a lifetime. The upside is that your role always has hope and room for growth. Never get discouraged if it is hard for you to connect with your children during their early childhood.

You can be their playmate, bringing fun and laughter. Play is a time to share closeness, affection, and stimulation. Through rough-and-tumble play, you can help your children develop important skills, such as impulse control, respect towards others, and confidence in their bodies.

Through affection you release oxytocin in your bodies. Oxytocin is also known as the "love hormone." It is linked to the bonding and attachment experiences between parents and children. Oxytocin makes you feel closer and more trusting of each other. It strengthens relationships and social skills. Consider affection as a boost to the mental health of everyone in your family.

Your attention is also a highly precious resource. A common complaint is that fathers are not fully present with their children. As 'doers,' fathers are used to a working environment with some problems to solve. However, your children will most likely just want you to **be** with them. This is the energy of the father Lover. They seek your unconditional presence, without an agenda of teaching or fixing.

How do you 'do' that?

Structure a special time with your child and let them know you will do whatever they want to do. Let them lead. For a child under the age of seven, set a maximum special time of thirty minutes without any distractions and no screens. Stick to the time. Do this ritual at least once a week.

As an engaged father, you will get to know your child well because you show interest in them and listen. You convey to your child that they matter to you. They will reciprocate it by admiring you as their father.

Mistakes of the father Lover

If you are an overactive father Lover, you may indulge your child's senses without having proper breaks, or you may provide them with fun times but no boundaries.

On the other hand, if you are an underactive father Lover, you will be distanced, disengaged, and unavailable.

The father Magician

As a father Magician, you recognize and understand the strong attachment between your wife and your children. You see her vulnerability and reactivity for what they are. When she seems to be affected by your children, you should offer her support, not judgment. Never underestimate the emotional toll on your wife if one of your children is not well. Your non-attached perspective in that situation is your strength. Your non-reactive approach helps to de-escalate any tension with the kids. If you respond with empathy by reflecting on and showing understanding of their feelings, you can calm everyone down.

You match your wife's 'way of the heart' with your 'way of the mind.' You explain, you reason, and you engage your child in problem-solving. You tease, provoke, and challenge them to think things through. When stuck, kids often turn to their mothers as the usual 'rescuers.' Mothers tend to help instantly because this is what their nurturing instincts dictate. Children may manipulate a situation to take advantage of this instinct. As a father Magician, you see beyond any instant gratification. You encourage your children to problem-solve and coach them on how to do it. You teach them to fish instead of giving them the fish. Your input helps your children to develop self-regulation, resilience, and self-reliance.

Acting as a coach, you inspire and encourage them to tap into their strengths. You motivate them to achieve their goals. As they grow towards independence, they increasingly turn to you because they intuitively recognize your valuable wisdom for coping with the 'real' world. You can become their mentor as they pursue a life of independence.

Mistakes by the father Magician

In the overactive state, you may constantly try to teach and coach them to the point that they lose interest in what you say. You may show little consideration towards their emotional state.

In the underactive state, you may present as reactive, confused, and emotional. You may get easily frustrated and angry when they resist you, as children normally do.

The father Warrior

In your role as a father Warrior, you balance and complement the energy of feminine motherhood more than in any of your other roles. Your wife tends to be protective of your children, and you challenge them. She may offer them softness and you offer toughness instead. She may be unconditionally accepting and forgiving of them, but you bring the 'real' world perspective to them, in which they pay the price for bad actions and gain rewards for hard work and good behavior.

You challenge your children and stretch them out of their comfort zone. You toughen them up and encourage them to be daring and take risks. You push, but you don't shame them! Like an enthusiastic coach on the sideline, you focus on encouragement, not criticism.

As a father Warrior, you build the kind of relationships with your children that they will have in the real world. Rather than a world without consequences, you instill your children with the realization that action always comes with some consequences. This realization is called responsibility. People in the real world will not care about their feelings as their mother does. Life presents the consequences matter-of-factly, and with your help, your children can learn not to take these consequences personally, but as an opportunity to learn and grow. This is the mindset of winners.[106]

Your child's pain is your wife's pain. Warrior fathers deal with such pains differently. They accept pain as part of life's journey. As a Warrior father, you will teach your children the lesson that accomplishing anything in life will require some sacrifice, some frustration, and some losses. No pain, no gain. You will frustrate them at times with your boundaries and you will upset them when you enforce consequences. Your children won't get everything they want and you must suspend their desires for instant gratification. Teach your child self-regulation instead, a skill that according to many studies predicts success and healthy living in later life.[107]

If your child plays the victim, challenge them to look at themselves, own their situation, take responsibility, and claim back their power. For example: "But why do you think the kids bully you and not others? Is there something you do to annoy them? And even if you never provoked the bully, what do you think you can do differently?" Model them on the basic Warrior code—"I am the agent for anything that happens to me in my life." Help them to build faith in their abilities to cope with life's challenges.

You may have noticed how your children behave differently when your wife is away and they are alone with you. This does not necessarily prove that your wife does something wrong and you do something right. Do not hold it against her! It is the nature of mother-child attachment. What it proves though is that children benefit from their time alone with you. They value your unique masculine energy. It should make them exert a bit more effort, act more independently, and display a bit more of their potential. With your no-nonsense Warrior approach, they will understand that they won't get away with anything easily. In other words, you provide them with a real-life experience. Therefore, it's important that you spend more time alone with your children. And if you convince your wife that this allows her more time and space for herself, then everyone wins.

Growing up without boundaries, challenges, or the need to consider others is a breeding ground for children to develop narcissistic traits: being demanding and exploitative, having a sense of entitlement, and feeling angry for not getting what they want. You don't need to study psychology to realize how excessive parental pampering and indulging lead to what has become a social epidemic of narcissism.[108] This happens when the masculine Warrior fails to balance the feminine nurturer.

Sadly, some mothers (out of their good hearts) often fail to see the damage caused by indulging children. And fathers fail to correct the trend out of convenience or fear of upsetting both mothers and kids. As a father Warrior, you do not seek fake harmony but step into the 'fire' to enforce your family rules.

Doing so will save your children from developing the highly undesirable traits of narcissism.

Mistakes of the father Warrior

In the overactive state, you may show poor understanding of your children's needs while too focused on outcomes. Showing low tolerance towards their mistakes, you may end up being critical, demanding, and even ruthless.

In the underactive state, you may be lenient, avoid enforcing consequences, and you may come across as too soft and too protective.

Case study – the father of Serena and Venus Williams

The story of the father of tennis players Serena and Venus Williams is told in the movie King Richard. (What a name! The movie came out just as I was finishing this book.) It gives us a good opportunity to illustrate our *Good Husband* model.

Richard, a father of 5 girls, exhibits the four roles in his fatherhood. As the father King, Richard leads with the clarity of his mission. He is clear with his values, his vision for the future success of his daughters when they were children, and his 'way'—hard work and discipline are required for them to be successful. He sticks to his way and principles in a manner perceived by others as too rigid and stubborn. He imposes his rules and authority. When a new coach introduced himself to his daughters when they were children by saying "I am Paul," he corrects him: "No, your name is Mr. Cohen."

As the father Lover, he shows affection and jokes with his girls. As the father Magician, he inspires them to have total belief in their abilities. He keeps evoking visions of their future success and instills an unwavering faith in them. At a crucial crossroads of her career, he encourages Venus to make her own decision. As a Warrior, he goes a long way to fight for the interests of his daughters and he sets clear boundaries for them.

When the girls brag after a win, he punishes them for not being humble. If he suspects some racism, he reacts strongly. While trying to protect his daughters from local thugs, he is bashed in front of them. Next came a powerful message. He returned to the car to drive his shocked and quiet girls back home. After a moment of silence, he said: "I didn't have a daddy to protect me, but these guys are going to respect you."

My father

As I finish writing this chapter, I remember my late father. At age seven, his father was murdered by Arabs in Yemen, and at age eight, he migrated with his older sister to the promised land of Israel. He reunited with his mother when he was a teenager, fighting in the War of Independence. He was acknowledged by army officers for his kindness.

We were five kids sharing a very small flat in a lower-class neighborhood of Tel Aviv. Mother was mentally unwell with frequent hospitalization. Our life was largely shaped by Father's religious practice. You wouldn't call him a typical King who created order with his authority, but our religious practice provided the order we needed. Religion was like a holding environment in the midst of chaos.

Father modeled integrity and humility. He was described by many as a righteous man. (righteous, and accepting of others!) It was clear to us all that his way was the moral path. My father was good as a Lover father. He fulfilled both parental roles for me—mother and father. His affection, warmth, kindness, and compassion still ring their tunes in my body. Reflecting on him brings tears to my eyes.

As a Magician, he used his amazing sense of humor to defuse tough situations and make us laugh. He provided us with guidance and inspiration through Biblical stories. He was non-reactive and rarely angry. Yet, my father was not strong as a Warrior. He was not assertive with my mother or other people. He was a typical 'nice guy' who avoided conflicts.

When I was eight, my father placed me and my sister in an institution for children from dysfunctional families. He cried. I felt betrayed and abandoned. Childhood from that moment on became a story of neglect, bullying, and helplessness. Those harrowing years honed my resilience and fighting spirit. I could become for my children the father Warrior that my father was not. Unlike my father, I didn't pray to God for help. I took action.

PRACTICE:

Reflect on how your father performed the four *Good Husband* roles.

Share your thoughts with your partner.

In what way would you like to do things similarly or differently with your children?

Which of the four roles do you currently do best and which one would you like to improve most?

The 'bad cop' story

Too many times I have heard men complaining about their role as the 'bad cop' in the family. They feel hurt and resentful for that. They perceive themselves as nurturing and caring fathers, but somehow they are seen by their families as perpetrators. These fathers have been caught in a hidden power game that involves three roles: victim, rescuer, and perpetrator. It is known as "The Drama Triangle."[109] Let me shed some light here.

The Drama Triangle is a model that explains the dysfunctional roles people play during conflicts. Each of the three roles represents a mindset—a way of thinking and behaving during conflicts. During this Drama Triangle, people are highly reactive. They are hypnotized by their social role. There is no hurry to 'wake up' and change because the roles come with some gains.

The victims feel victimized, helpless, and powerless, but their gains are sympathy, support, feeling righteous, and avoiding action and responsibility.

The rescuers gain a sense of power and meaning from their rescuing mission. It makes them avoid their issues and vulnerabilities. Their focus is on others, not themselves. (I suspect this was my initial motivation to pursue a career as a psychologist...) Helping and advocating for others is empowering for both the receiver and the giver.

The perpetrators attempt to achieve their goals by trying to control, intimidate, or hurt others. They are often angry, defensive, or aggressive. They gain a sense of control and power and often get what they want.

In terms of relationships, the main beneficiaries of this Drama Triangle are the victim and rescuer because their tie is strengthened by it. They are in fact co-dependent, and the perpetrator unintentionally strengthens their bond. Perpetrators are the 'bad guys' that we like to dislike. They make us look good and righteous.

Fathers are the traditional perpetrators who make mothers rescue their children. Here lies the origin of the 'bad cop' story. The child protests to win the mother's sympathy and closeness. The mother, in turn, comes to the rescue, too keen to show her love and care. They both create a powerful and very rewarding subconscious contract. To strengthen their bond, they may use the father as the 'bad cop.'

But what if it goes in the other direction and the child turns to the father for rescue? Then the marital relationship is at risk. Mothers may not tolerate the status of being seen as the perpetrator. This is painful as it attacks their self-image as a loving parent. Such mothers often take their frustration out on their husbands, or worse; they prefer to separate and take the children with them. The Court may reinstate the traditional narrative of fathers as perpetrators.

Let's take a closer look at your role in this drama. The most common situation is when you are trying to discipline your child or set a boundary, and your wife over-rules you, or worse, intervenes to rescue your child. You feel disempowered and increasingly frustrated and angry. The next time your child begins to whine, you recognize it as a signal to your wife as the rescuer. You get even angrier, you react, and the situation escalates quickly. Your wife comes running to the rescue and you have all just been locked into the Drama Triangle.

Here is your way out.

As a Magician, see it for what it is. Recognize the Drama Triangle. Become aware of how the manipulation works. Name it. Say something to your wife, such as "I am afraid we are locked into a drama here which is not helping any of us. I don't enjoy being the bad cop..." Keep calm and centered. Encourage her to reconsider her strategy by asking "Are you sure this is helping our child?"

As a King, set a new order that will prevent the drama. That is, agree with your wife on how best to respond to your child's whining, tantrums, or crying. Raise her awareness of your child's need for security, and the importance of rules and boundaries to meet this need. Ask her to align with you so you don't confuse your child. Remind her what is in your child's best interests in the long run.

As a Lover, acknowledge your wife's sensitivity to your child's pain. Say to her softly, "Please trust me on that..." Reassure her that you are helping your child and come from a place of care, rather than anger. Also explain how giving in to your child now may result in worse outcomes for everyone later. Get your wife to see that you actually support her.

As a Warrior, ask her calmly to let you handle the situation. Warn her that if she intervenes, it makes the matter worse for everyone—you will be upset with each other and your child won't get what they want. Be clear and calm with your boundaries. Don't let the 'victim' get away with anything. If you resign with a sense of defeat, you betray your mission. This is your chance to model assertive behavior for your child and encourage their resilience and independence. Be prepared to accept protests from both mother and child! Don't argue with them. As a Warrior, you are a man of action, not words.

> ## PRACTICE:
>
> **Reflect for a moment on how the drama pans out in your family.**
>
> **Consider sharing this segment with your partner and discuss how you both wish to learn from it.**

The dark side of parenting

Parenting is a story of love towards our children. However, this love story also has a dark side. Children can be used and exploited by their parents for their own personal needs.

In the old days, many parents needed their children to work on farms. Today, children can be used in conflicts between parents or for any other emotional needs. The horrible stories about fathers who kill their children to punish their mothers reveal something about the dark side in men's psyche—treating children as a means to an end. For these men, the trophy is the woman, and children are a way to own her. This approach is still common in some cultures. If their wives leave, these men lose their purpose, the ground they stand on, and interest in their children. One of my clients asked his father why he disappeared from his life fifteen years ago when he was three. "Your mother didn't let me see you," was the victimhood-driven answer. As you read this, ask yourself how determined you are to fight and care for your children if your wife wants to separate tomorrow.

The dark side of female parenting is when women use their kids to fulfill their needs to feel loved and worthy. They experience their kids as some kind of extension of themselves. These women take ownership of them as **their** 'territory' and sideline the children's fathers. For example, a mother may speak about "my kids," not "our kids." She expects the father to share the parenting tasks, but when it comes to parenting rights, she may treat him as disposable. If she does, we may see that in how she talks about parenting in the case of looming divorce. Sadly, she may find support in the way society treats fathers in some parts of the world.

This mother's dark side may appear in a subtle way. If the father does his job so well that the children are attached to him, this might backfire. She may resent it because it comes at the expense of her closeness to the kids. In her role perception as the mother, she is the critical figure your children should be more attached to, and to whom they should turn if they are distressed. As her resentment grows, she may consider that the only option to win access to the hearts of her children is separating from their father. This is an inadvertent consequence of being a good father, but not connected to your children's mother as your wife.

Parenting inside out

Both parents in a family may bring their subconscious needs and childhood wounds to their parenting experience. From the dark basement of their inner child, 'gremlins' may emerge to sabotage the marriage. Too often I have witnessed partners who are more keen on attacking each other than showing care for their inner child. They fail to consider that their own inner child needs attention and love.

Caring for and healing your inner child is a gift for your children. Parenting is a task that works simultaneously on the inside and the outside. To provide care, empathy and understanding to your children, start with doing these things for your inner child. More than anything else, your children want to see you and your wife happy and calm as parents. Parenting is done by 'being' before 'doing'—by working the heart before the hands. Therefore, your well-being as parents matters far more for your children than the quality of any parenting advice you get.

So, give your kids connected parents, not a bigger TV screen. It's better to pay a babysitter than pay a marriage counselor. Nurturing your relationship is the best thing you will do for your children. Be a good father by being a *Good Husband*. In a good marriage, you both nurture these other two hidden children in your family.

Your takeaway messages

- Fatherhood is forever a role in the making. It evolves and changes over the years and it requires your conscious intentions.

- Your fatherhood qualities complement your wife's motherhood qualities. She lays the foundations for your children's security and self-love, and you lay the foundations for their competence and self-directedness.

- The 'father effect' is a proven and uniquely positive impact fathers have on their children's well-being.

- Involved fathers make a big difference by balancing the qualities of the feminine (nurturing and providing affection) with the masculine (challenging and enforcing consequences).

- As a father King, you will give your family the order they need to feel secure.

- As a father Lover, you will relate to your children's feelings, be present and show them affection.

- As a father Magician, you will bring the non-attached male perspective to balance the strong reactivity between mothers and children.

- As a father Warrior, you will bring the experience of the 'real world' to your children—challenges, boundaries, and consequences. You will stretch them beyond their secure base—out of their comfort zone.

- The 'bad cop' story results from the social power game known as the Drama Triangle. Be aware of this game and learn to respond to it effectively.

- Your parenting is largely affected by your inner child—your emotional self. The best gift for your children is for both you and your wife to invest in this 'inner child.' Be a good father by being a *Good Husband* and taking good care of your relationship

10
THE GOOD
ENOUGH HUSBAND

"To claim the truths about who we are, and the very imperfect nature of our lives, we have to be willing to give ourselves a break, and appreciate the beauty of our cracks or imperfections. To be kinder and gentler with ourselves and each other."

— **Brené Brown, Daring Greatly**

This concluding chapter will recap our *Good Husband* model and suggest a gentle way to integrate it into your marriage. The nature of projects such as ours is that we aim high and aspire to be the best possible version of ourselves. However, reality forever lags behind our ideals. This eternal gap between the 'real' and 'ideal' may create some frustration. Some people cope with this frustrating gap by applying judgment and criticism to hasten the change (see Chapter One).

However, the approach in our *Good Husband* project is one of empathy, understanding, and acceptance towards the 'real'— our vulnerabilities and flaws as human beings, both men and women. Perfectionism is not only a bad idea, but it's very toxic. Having our standards too high often leads to disappointment, judgment, and the too familiar feeling of shame.

The intention of our project is to inspire you with possibilities, rather than set lofty standards that may cause more self-doubts or criticism from your partner and society as a whole. To temper any battle with internal and external critics, we need a softer approach of 'good enough.' But before I suggest such an approach let's recap our model.

The Good Husband recap

The *Good Husband* model is based on four classically masculine roles—King, Lover, Magician, and Warrior. You do not want to take these roles too seriously. You are the director of your masculine roles! Use each role just when you need it the most. Ask "What role can serve me best here?" Be prepared to swap hats easily. Getting into a role is like acting a character; to act a character well, you need to understand how it thinks and feels. Chapters eight and nine illustrated how each masculine 'character' thinks and operates.

Let's refresh your memory by briefly recapping how each role works.

- **As a King, you will create order.**

    Creating order requires the most advanced functioning of our brain. As a King, you are responsible for the future of your family. You make sure that they have the conditions necessary for flourishing. Their most basic need is security.

    You lead with intentions rather than reactions. Your power lies in your words. You mean what you say. Your family will hear you talking about values, principles, rules, agreements, roles, accountability, and any other idea that helps create discipline and order. At the same time, you remain open to their feedback and influence.

- **As a Lover, you will cultivate connection.**

  For close relationships, connection is like water to a plant. It dies without it. It flounders when there is little of it. Unresolved conflicts mostly reflect a loss of connection. In such moments, the Lover in you is called up. You don't withdraw or attack, but remain engaged.

  Cultivating connection is your most effective way to make your marriage resilient and stable. You enhance connection through affection, sharing, listening, and fun activities.

- *As a Magician, you will transform reactivity.*

  Marital troubles originate in our reactive brain. Reactivity is particularly high in family relationships. The closer people are, the more reactive they become—which is why mother-baby relationships are the most reactive.

  To temper intense emotions, you will use the power of your scientific and reflective skills. Your family needs your perspective, empathy, and mindful capacities: observing, asking, wondering, accepting, and reflecting.

- **As a Warrior, you will command respect.**

  The opposite of respect is contempt, the strongest predictor of divorce. Getting the Warrior role right is the most urgent task for modern men.

  Men lose respect when they avoid or attack during conflicts. A Warrior will engage, face issues, and take action to resolve them. If treated badly, he swiftly sets boundaries to command respect.

The learning mindset of the 'good enough'

Regardless of how well you perform as a husband, having a learning mindset is an attitude that instills hope in everyone. It means that you are continuously learning and becoming. A learning mindset is your ultimate 'ticket' to the 'good enough husbands club.'

Learning is the language life 'speaks' to us. Life regularly gives us information to learn from. One type of information flows from the past—feedback and the consequences of our actions. The other type of information is about the future, with new ideas and possibilities.

A learning mindset enables you to be more engaged with life than with your mind, your stories, or your ego. Learning is always done in the 'now.' You are in a continuous 'conversation' with life rather than your guarded self-image. Your system is open. You don't need to defend anything. You absorb, digest, and adapt. This ability to adapt is the mechanism underlying the evolutionary principle of 'survival of the fittest.' The fittest are the best learners. Rather than attempting a failing strategy time and time again, people with a learning mindset try something different. Since they experiment more, the fittest have more potential outcomes to choose from.

When learning is your guiding principle, you constantly evolve, rather than revolve. For your wife, it means there is always an open window for her messages to enter. If you have read the book to this point, you have learned much. You are a natural learner if you have completed 2–3 of the practice exercises. Well done!

What does a learning mindset mean?

A learning mindset means an attitude of openness and curiosity towards your experiences. Rather than judgment, resistance, and control, you treat challenging experiences (failures, conflicts, fears, loss of power) as an opportunity for your learning and growth. Let's look at the qualities that are associated with the learning mindset.

Openness

You are curious about new ideas, and open to feedback on your actions. You allow life to present possibilities to you, and to teach you matter-of-factly. You perceive yourself as dynamic and open, rather than static and fixed.

Self-Acceptance

Having a learning mindset means having profound self-acceptance. You accept yourself as you are, but acknowledge where you might be lacking some skills or knowledge.

Having an agenda for improving your skills is very different to changing yourself! Recall the mental bug of shame. This bug leads to perfectionism, anxiety, and defensiveness, three notorious enemies of learning.

Humility

You are humble enough to acknowledge that you don't know or understand everything, or that you need to upskill. A learning mindset does not worry about self-image or self-worth, because you are not defined by the amount of knowledge in your brain.

To stop a defensive ego from arresting your growth, see your worth in what you are becoming rather than in what you own. Your values, vision, and potential offer better prospects for defining who you are.

Courage

Learning is stepping into the unknown. The unknown often provokes fears that keep us in our comfort zone. It takes some daring to step out of your comfort zone.

Resilience

If all experiences (both pleasant and unpleasant) are here to teach you something, then you only see them as an opportunity for your growth. This is an attitude of hope. Even in the worst times, your quest for a lesson continues. Despair happens when people don't realize what there is for them to learn.

Sense of agency

As a learner, you take responsibility for anything that happens. This is not a position of guilt, but of taking control of your future because learning is only used in the future.

Barriers to learning

Too often I see partners who are stuck in a cycle of attack/defend. They arrive at counseling wounded so deeply that their only wish is not to get hurt anymore. This survival mode sets them up to protect themselves from further blame, criticism, rejection, and disappointment.

Recall the attachment brain. If there is no security, then there is no exploring behavior. Like acrobats in the circus, to dare you need a safety net to hold you. This safety net is not there when partners' trust in each other is badly damaged. It makes the process of learning very difficult. They need to restore trust and security first.

Without security, it is harder to explore and learn together. Partners are not open to feedback if they feel hurt, judged, or rejected by the other. In such conditions, doing the learning on your own promises better outcomes. Most of my relationship counseling is done with individuals. In a safe and accepting environment, people are more receptive to new ideas and more open to coaching.

Integrating a learning mindset into your marriage

For the 'good enough husband,' let's ask what the minimum is, not the maximum, you can do. Guided by this question, consider three basic tasks for each masculine role.

As a King, your purpose is to create order. To meet the good enough standard in this role, you will:

a) have your own life in order. That is, you are reliable and predictable for your family. You will have no issues with a bad temper, addictions, or uncontrolled behaviors.

b) discuss your family values and encourage everyone to live by them.

c) enforce the family values on your children by applying the desired authoritative approach that balances warmth with demands.

As a Lover, your purpose is to build a connection. To meet the good enough standard in this role, you will:

a) make more attempts at engagement than attempts at withdrawal both during and after conflicts.

b) initiate activities that strengthen your friendship and enrich your emotional bank account.

c) show affection. Touch your wife a few times throughout the day to let her know she is desired.

As a Magician, your purpose is to transform reactivity. To meet the good enough standard in this role, you will:

a) manage your temper and emotions reasonably well. That is, your reactivity won't provoke fear in your wife or children.

b) respond to her complaints with some curiosity instead of defensiveness.

c) bring a scientific approach to parenting issues. Search for what works.

As a Warrior, your purpose is to command respect. To meet the good enough standard in this role, you will:

a) hold a steady job in which you fulfill your talents and provide for your family.

b) respond to conflicts with engagement, but without compromising your self-respect.

c) respond swiftly to any attempt to hurt a family member, including yourself.

Since your wife is ultimately the person who is experiencing your husbandhood, you will need her feedback for your learning process. So let's turn her into your coach. She knows how well you do on your masculine tasks, and can tell you where you could improve. Yet, as you may recall, most of the time, the feedback partners share is nothing but reaction. Reactivity means repeating the past rather than shaping the future. It means interpretations and memories. This is the 'noise' in the system.

To reduce the noise of reactivity and focus on the future, I have designed a practice of *intentional learning*. With intentional learning, you will proactively seek feedback based on experiences rather than on distorted perceptions or interpretations.

The following intentional learning practice will conclude our journey.

PRACTICE:

Show your wife the list of 'good enough' husband tasks, and then go through the following steps. Approaching the exercise playfully might be useful for you both.

Step 1
Discuss which of the above twelve tasks you may need to improve on. With your King, you create an intention of learning and openness to receiving her feedback.

Step 2
Ask her to rate on a scale of 1–10 how well you perform this task at the moment.

Discuss and agree on the meaning of the number for you both. Store the number she gave you on your phone.

With your Lover, you tell her how much she matters to you, how much you care about her, and how committed you are to your relationship.

Step 3
As you try to improve, ask her at least twice a week to share her re-evaluation on a scale of 1–10 via text messages.

Store these numbers on your phone.

If she agrees, ask her to explain the numbers.

With your Magician, you observe and collect data like a scientist.

Step 4
After 2–3 weeks of this experiment, sit down with your wife to reflect on the experiment and share what you learned from her feedback.

With your Warrior, you set a goal and take action to complete it.

It's important to understand that as much as you try to learn and grow, there is no guarantee that your wife shares the same openness to learning. She could be very defensive. Some personalities are highly resistant to any learning.

As a good learner, listen carefully to what life is 'telling' you about the prospect of change. Sometimes, the best thing you can do is accept the situation, grieve, and let go of some of your dreams. It might even mean that separation is the better option for you. You will know it is if your desire to separate comes not from anger, but from a sense of profound acceptance of your sad reality.

What about couples therapy?

I wish I could speak with more enthusiasm about this form of therapy. Too many factors need to come together for it to create success: personality issues and how they interact with one another, the depth and longevity of the wounds, the level of commitment, and the therapist's experience and approach. And there is also a level of anti-male bias among many couples therapists who are mostly females.

As a rule, couples therapy is not essential as long as you are engaged in learning (for example, open to talk, receptive to feedback, and accountable). The majority of couples therapy referrals are initiated by women who are worried about their marriages. They often hope to open the process of learning for both partners. I recommend you respond positively to your wife's suggestion for therapy if she makes it. You will show her that you care and are open to learning.

However, if you suggest couples therapy and your wife resists, then you should certainly focus your efforts on doing the learning on your own. Just as you hopefully have benefited from this book, you will benefit from counseling for yourself.

When you call a counselor, either for you both or just for yourself, I suggest assessing them by their answers to these two questions:

1. "How will you help me with problem x?"

    A good quality answer will offer some perspectives on how to understand the issue and some possible strategies and tools that might help. You want to know that the therapist has something to offer.

2. "What should I expect to see and experience during the session?"

    A good quality answer will describe the processes and techniques that the therapist will use. It should alarm you if the therapist sounds elusive, too general, or defensive. Open and generous answers will reflect the therapist's wisdom and respect towards you.

Takeaway messages

- Standards that are too high often lead to judgment and shame. The answer is empathy and acceptance towards one's vulnerabilities and flaws.

- The 'good enough' is characterized by engaging in a process of learning. A learning mindset creates hope and resilience.

- A learning mindset means openness, self-acceptance, and a sense of agency.

- Insecurities in relationships block learning. To facilitate learning try to build security first.

- Use the Intentional learning practice above to improve your masculine roles.

MY PARTING WORDS

You embarked on this journey to address the gap between your ideals of being a family man who makes his wife happy and the harsh reality of conflicts, loss of power, and looming threats of divorce. My promise was to provide you with a roadmap and practical tools so that you can express your masculine strengths to benefit your family. I hope the book has lived up to that promise.

Learning to be a better husband is a noble cause. There is no promotion or salary increase; even appreciation is not guaranteed. At times, it may be just the opposite. Being a better husband is about your family, so any investment in your role is an investment in your family, and therefore, in society as a whole! You should be proud of yourself for striving to achieve it, and we as a society should show you our support and appreciation.

I am immensely grateful to men like you who are open to learning from me and who benefit from the gifts I share. When you read 'my story' in the introduction to this book, I indicated that you would find hints about what helped me make the journey from a helpless child to where I am today. I hope I have given you enough hints. Love for others has been my secret. It has empowered me! It has given me meaning. With each gift I give away, I feel richer, stronger, and only more grateful.

I will continue to support men like you via my website www.thegoodhusband.online. Join the community, share, ask questions, learn more and teach me what I should know. I will be happy to read your responses via the email hagaiavisar@gmail.com and I will respond to common questions via the website.

ACKNOWLEDGEMENTS

I could not have developed the wisdom I shared in this book without the trust and loyalty of my clients over the years. Some of them encouraged me to write this book. I am immensely grateful for them all.

Thank you, my early readers, who generously shared feedback to help me get the right tone for the book.

Since English is not my mother tongue, I needed much help from my editors: John Coomer, who helped me navigate the complex issue of language and cultural nuances, and Justin Parry, who shared insightful comments and corrections that helped me polish the messages. Thank you both.

And finally, thank you, Judy, my ex-wife, and my children Lia, and Itai, for your care and moral support.

ENDNOTES

1   Warren Farrell (2001). *The myth of male power* (Berkley Pub Group).

2   Warren Farrell and John Gray (2018). *The boy crisis: why our boys are struggling and what we can do about it* (BenBella Books).

3   Jim Macnamara (2006). *Media and male identity, the making and remaking of men.* https://www.researchgate.net/publication/320691279_Media_and_Male_Identity_The_Making_and_Remaking_of_Men.

4   Helen Pluckrose and James Lindsay (2020). *Cynical theories: how activist scholarship made everything about race, gender, and identity—and why this harms everybody* (Pitchstone Publishing).

5   American Psychological Association (2018). *APA guidelines for psychological practice with men.* https://www.apa.org/about/policy/boys-men-practice-guidelines.pdf (page 11).

6   Quillette (2019). *Twelve scholars respond to the APA's guidance for treating men and boys.* https://quillette.com/2019/02/04/psychologists-respond-to-the-apas-guidance-for-treating-men-and-boys/.

7   Independent Man (2019). *Experts respond to APA guidelines for men & boys.* https://youtu.be/1mctb81ksMA.

8   Shawn T. Smith (2019). *APA's war on masculinity.* https://www.youtube.com/watch?v=WO93hW_uVao.

9   Stephanie Pappas (2019). *APA issues first-ever guidelines for practice with men and boys.* https://www.apa.org/monitor/2019/01/ce-corner.

10 Jim Macnamara (2006). *Media and Male Identity, The Making and Remaking of Men.* https://www.researchgate.net/publication/320691279_Media_and_Male_Identity_The_Making_and_Remaking_of_Men.

11 Paul Nathanson and Katherine Young (2006). *Spreading misandry: the teaching of contempt for men in popular culture* (McGill-Queen's University Press).

12 ABC News (2017). *Google fires employee who blamed gender diversity on 'biological causes.'* https://www.abc.net.au/news/2017-08-08/google-employee-behind-anti-diversity-memo-fired/8785596.

13 Jess Butcher (2018). *Is modern feminism starting to undermine itself?* https://www.youtube.com/watch?v=lgIgytWyo_A.

14 Warren Farrell and John Gray (2018). *The boy crisis: why our boys are struggling and what we can do about it* (BenBella Books).

15 Lisa J. Warren (2021). *The invisible cage:* Psychology's role in the criminalization of coercive control (Australian Psychological Society). https://psychology.org.au/for-members/publications/inpsych/2021/april-may-issue-2/the-invisible-cage.

16 Evelyn Rae (2021). *Police resent enforcing unjust feminist laws – former police officer speaks out (Bettina Arndt).* https://www.youtube.com/watch?v=wzs-lFuNluw.

17 Helen Smith (2014). *Men on strike: why men are boycotting marriage, fatherhood and the american dream* (Encounter Books).

18 Helen Pluckrose and James Lindsay (2020). Cynical theories: how activist scholarship made everything about race, gender, and identity—and why this harms everybody (Pitchstone Publishing).

19 Carole Hooven (2021). *The story of testosterone, the hormone that dominates and divides us* (Henry Holt and Co.), page 25.

20   The Australian (2021). *Battle of the sexes is a war no one can win.* https://www.theaustralian.
com.au/inquirer/battle-of-the-sexes-is-a-war-no-one-can-win/news-story/8b7b53c430c16a83b
25c04c1be25127b.

21   Kristin Donnelly and Jean Twenge (2017). *Masculine and feminine traits on the bem sex-role
inventory, 1993–2012: a Cross-Temporal Meta-Analysis* (Springer). https://www.researchgate.
net/publication/301330037_Masculine_and_Feminine_Traits_on_the_Bem_Sex-Role_
Inventory_1993-2012_a_Cross-Temporal_Meta-Analysis.

22   David Buss (2016). *The evolution of desire: strategies of human mating* (Basic Books), page 331.

23   John Gottman, (1991). Predicting the longitudinal course of marriages. *Journal of Marital and
Family Therapy,* 17(1), 3–7. https://psycnet.apa.org/record/2012-18290-001.

24   Richard Lippa (2005). *Gender, nature, and nurture* (Routledge).

25   Vicki Helgeson (2020). *Psychology of Gender* (Routledge).

26   David Buss (2019). *Evolutionary psychology: the new science of the mind* (Routledge).

27   Amy Wharton (2011). *The sociology of gender.* (Wiley-Blackwell).

28   Stefan Horlacher (Editor) (2005). *Configuring masculinity in theory and literary practice.* (Brill
Rodopi). https://library.oapen.org/bitstream/handle/20.500.12657/43453/external_content.
pdf?sequence=1.

29   Marianne Walters, Betty Carter, Peggy Papp, and Olga Silverstein (1991). *The invisible web:
gender patterns in family relationships* (The Guilford Press).

30   John Gottman (2010). *The marriage clinic: a scientifically based marital therapy* (Norton).

31   Richard Lippa (2005). *Gender, nature, and nurture* (Routledge).

32   Richard Lippa (2005). *Gender, nature, and nurture* (Routledge).

33   National Geographic Documentary Films (2021). *The Rescue.*

34   David Buss, ibid.

35   Vicki Helgeson (2020). *Psychology of Gender* (Routledge).

36   Carnegie Hero Fund Commission. https://www.carnegiehero.org/heroes/search-heroes/.

37   David Buss (2019). Evolutionary psychology: the new science of the mind (Routledge).

38   Michael S. Sand, William Fisher, and Boehringer-Ingelheim Pharma. (2007) Erectile
dysfunction and constructs of masculinity and quality of life in the multinational Men's
Attitudes to Life Events and Sexuality (MALES) study. *Journal of Sexual Medicine,* 5(3):
583–594.

39   Kristin Donnelly and Jean Twenge (2017). *Masculine and feminine traits on the bem sex-role
inventory, 1993–2012: a Cross-Temporal Meta-Analysis* (Springer). https://www.researchgate.
net/publication/301330037_Masculine_and_Feminine_Traits_on_the_Bem_Sex-Role_
Inventory_1993-2012_a_Cross-Temporal_Meta-Analysis.

40   Vicki Helgeson (2020). *Psychology of gender* (Routledge).

41   Robert Moore and Douglas Gillette (1991). *King, warrior, magician, lover: rediscovering the
archetypes of the mature masculine* (HarperCollins US).

42   Carole Hooven (2021). *The story of testosterone, the hormone that dominates and divides us*
(Henry Holt and Co.).

43   Carmen P. McLean, Anu Asnaani, Brett Litz, and Stefan Hofmann (2011). Gender differences
in anxiety disorders: prevalence, course of illness, comorbidity and burden of illness. *Journal
of Psychiatry Research.* Aug; 45(8): 1027–1035. https://www.ncbi.nlm.nih.gov/pmc/articles/
PMC3135672/.

44   Carol Brayne (2016). A systematic review of reviews on the prevalence of anxiety disorders
in adult populations. *Journal of Brain and Behavior* https://onlinelibrary.wiley.com/doi/
full/10.1002/brb3.497.

45   World Health Organization. (2002). *Gender and mental health.* https://www.who.int/gender/
other_health/genderMH.pdf.

46 Louann Brizendine (2007). *The female brain* (Harmony).

47 Carmen P. McLean, Anu Asnaani, Brett Litz, and Stefan Hofmann (2011). Gender differences in anxiety disorders: prevalence, course of illness, comorbidity and burden of illness. *Journal of Psychiatry Research. Aug;* 45(8): 1027–1035. https://www.ncbi.nlm.nih.gov/pmc/articles/PMC3135672/.

48 Better Health Channel (2022). *Mental illness statistics.* https://www.betterhealth.vic.gov.au/health/servicesandsupport/mental-illness-statistics#mental-illness-and-increased-risk-of-suicide.

49 University of Western Australia (2022). *Common mental health issues.* https://www.safety.uwa.edu.au/health-wellbeing/health/psychological/common-mental-health-issues#.

50 Catherine Hakim. Erotic capital (2010). *European Sociological Review,* 26(5): October 2010, 499–518. https://doi.org/10.1093/esr/jcq014.

51 Catherine Hakim, ibid.

52 Robert Glover (2003). *No more Mr. Nice guy: a proven plan for getting what you want in love, sex, and life* (Running Press).

53 Richard Lippa (2005). *Gender, nature, and nurture* (Routledge).

54 Daniel Kahneman (2021). *Noise: a flaw in human judgment* (Little, Brown Spark).

55 John Gottman and Nan Silver (2000). *The seven principles for making marriage work* (Harmony Books), 113.

56 David Buss (2016). *The evolution of desire: strategies of human mating* (Basic Books).

57 TEDx Talks (2018). *The healing power of love and intimacy.* Dean Ormish. https://www.youtube.com/watch?v=KhbI4Aks1Wo

58 David Buss (2016). *The evolution of desire: strategies of human mating* (Basic Books), 238.

59 John Gottman and Nan Silver (2000). *The seven principles for making marriage work* (Harmony Books).

60 Sue Johnson (2013). *Love sense: the revolutionary new science of romantic relationships* (Little, Brown Spark).

61 Andrew Christensen and Christopher Heavey (1990). Gender and social structure in the demand/withdraw pattern of marital conflict. *Journal of Personality and Social Psychology,* 59(1), Jul 1990, 73–81.

62 Barbara Fredrickson (2009). *Positivity: top-notch research reveals the 3-to-1 ratio that will change your life* (Harmony).

63 Deborah Tannen (2013). *You just don't understand: women and men in conversation* (William Morrow Paperbacks).

64 John Gottman and Nan Silver (2000). *The seven principles for making marriage work* (Harmony Books).

65 Louann Brizendine (2007). *The female brain* (Harmony).

66 David Buss (2016). *The evolution of desire: strategies of human mating* (Basic Books), 281.

67 Esther Perel (2007). *Mating in captivity: unlocking erotic intelligence* (Harper Paperbacks), 51.

68 Martin Seligman (2012). *Flourish: a visionary new understanding of happiness and well-being.* (Atria Books).

69 Bronnie Ware (2012). *The top five regrets of the dying: a life transformed by the dearly departing* (Hay House).

70 Gregg Jacobs (2003). *The ancestral mind: reclaim the power* (Viking Press).

71 John Gottman (2010). *The marriage clinic: a scientifically based marital therapy* (Norton), 84.

72 Kateri McRae, Kevin N. Ochsner, Iris B. Mauss, John J. D. Gabrieli, and James J. Gross (2008). Gender differences in emotion regulation: an fMRI study of cognitive reappraisal. *Group Process & Intergroup Relations.* 2008 April; 11(2): 143–162. https://www.ncbi.nlm.nih.gov/pmc/articles/PMC5937254/pdf/nihms131942.pdf

73 Scott Miller, Mark Hubble, and Daryl Chow (2020). *Better results: using deliberate practice to improve therapeutic effectiveness* (American Psychological Association).

74 Carol Pearson (1998). *The hero within: six archetypes we live by* (HarperCollins), 193.

75 Daniel Siegel (2007). *The mindful brain: reflection and attunement in the cultivation of well-being* (W.W. Norton & Company), 180.

76 John Gottman and Nan Silver (2000). *The seven principles for making marriage work* (Harmony Books).

77 Eckhart Tolle (2004). *The power of now: a guide to spiritual enlightenment* (New World Library).

78 Daniel Siegel (2007). *The mindful brain: reflection and attunement in the cultivation of well-being* (W.W. Norton & Company).

79 Daniel Kahneman (2013). *Thinking fast and slow* (Farrar, Straus, and Giroux).

80 Navaz Habib (2019). *Activate your vagus nerve: unleash your body's natural ability to heal* (Ulysses Press).

81 Carol Pearson (1998). *The hero within: six archetypes we live by* (HarperCollins), 195.

82 David Buss (2019). *Evolutionary psychology: the new science of the mind* (Routledge).

83 Jack Donovan (2012). *The Way of Men* (Dissonant Hum).

84 Greg Lukianoff (2018). *The coddling of the American mind: how good intentions and bad ideas are setting up a generation for failure* (Penguin Press).

85 Domestic Violence Fact Sheet (2022). *Male victims of intimate partner violence* (National Coalition Against Domestic Violence). https://ncadv.org/STATISTICS.

86 Evelyn Rae (2021). *Police resent enforcing unjust feminist laws—former police officer speaks out (Bettina Arndt)*. https://www.youtube.com/watch?v=wzs-lFuNluw.

87 Personal Safety Survey (2016). *Experience of partner emotional abuse*. Australian Bureau of Statistics. https://www.abs.gov.au/statistics/people/crime-and-justice/personal-safety-australia/latest-release#experience-of-partner-violence.

88 Murray Straus, Sherry Hamby, Sue Boney-McCoy, and David Sugarman. (1996). The revised conflict tactics scales (cts2): development and preliminary psychometric data. *Journal of Family Issues* - J FAM ISS. 17. 283–316. 10.1177/019251396017003001.

89 Erin Pizzey (1998). *The emotional terrorist and the violence-prone.* (Commoners Publishing).

90 Ann Silvers (2014). *Abuse of men by women: it happens, it hurts, and it's time to get real about it* (Silvers Publishing).

91 Philip Cook (2009). *Abused men: the hidden side of domestic violence*, 2nd edition (Praeger).

92 Bettina Arndt (2018). *#MenToo* (Wilkinson Publishing).

93 Bettina Arndt. *#MenToo* https://www.youtube.com/user/bettinaarndtaus.

94 Carol Dweck (2007). *Mindset: the new psychology of success* (Ballantine Books).

95 David Buss (2016). *The evolution of desire: strategies of human mating* (Basic Books), 282.

96 Jordan B. Peterson (2018). *Twelve rules for life: an antidote to chaos* (Random House), 62.

97 John Gottman and Nan Silver (2000). *The seven principles for making marriage work* (Harmony Books).

98 Warren Farrell and John Gray (2018). *The boy crisis: why our boys are struggling and what we can do about it* (BenBella Books).

99 Sarah Allen and Kerry Daly (2002). *The effects of father involvement: a summary of the research evidence* (Newsletter of the Father Involvement Initiative—Ontario Network, Volume 1, Fall).

100 Jessica Ball (2011). *Father involvement in Canada—an emerging movement* (Journal of Childhood Education). https://www.researchgate.net/publication/254296083_Father_Involvement_in_Canada_An_Emerging_Movement

101 World Health Organization (2007). Fatherhood and health outcomes in europe: a summary report. (WHO Regional Office for Europe).

102 Warren Farrell and John Gray (2018). *The boy crisis: why our boys are struggling and what we can do about it* (BenBella Books).

103 Jessica Ball (2011). *Father involvement in Canada—an emerging movement* (Journal of Childhood Education). https://www.researchgate.net/publication/254296083_Father_Involvement_in_Canada_An_Emerging_Movement

104 Warren Farrell and John Gray (2018). *The boy crisis: why our boys are struggling and what we can do about it* (BenBella Books), 114.

105 Sofie Kuppens and Eva Ceulemans (2019). Parenting styles: a closer look at a well-known concept. *Journal of Child and Family Studies* 28(1): 168–181.

106 Carol Dweck (2007). *Mindset: the new psychology of success* (Ballantine Books).

107 D. A. Robson, M. S. Allen, and S. J. Howard (2020). *Self-regulation in childhood as a predictor of future outcomes: A meta-analytic review. Psychological Bulletin*, Online First 1-31.

108 Jean Twenge and Keith Campbell (2010). *The narcissism epidemic: living in the age of entitlement* (Atria).

109 Stephen Karpman (2014). *A game free life—the definitive book on the drama triangle by the originator and author* (Drama Triangle Publications).

Manufactured by Amazon.com.au
Sydney, New South Wales, Australia